I0547780

Skyline
2014

Cyberworld Publishing

www.CyberworldPublishing.com

This book is copyright © Olivia Stowe 2014
First published by Cyberworld Publishing in 2014
Cover design by S Bush © 2014
Cover photo: manipulated, Skyline Drive Copyright:Camrocker
E-book ISBN: 978-1-922187-86-4
Print ISBN: 978-1-922187-87-1
All rights reserved

No part of this book may be reproduced in any form, except for the inclusion of brief quotations in a review or article, without written permission from the author or publisher.

Cyberworld Publishing
Jindalee St
Toronto, NSW, 2283
Australia

Skyline
2014

An Anthology of
Prose and Poetry by
Central Virginia Writers

Olivia Stowe, ed.

Table of Contents

Prose Nonfiction

On Writing/Publishing

Introduction

Skyline 2014, an annual publisher's anthology produced by Cyberworld Publishing, showcases the prose and poetry talent of Central Virginia writers, using the writing contest winners of the members of the Blue Ridge Writers Chapter of the Virginia Writers Club as a base and adding invited works by established Central Virginia writers. Central Virginia is so richly blessed as the home base of best-selling authors that it's sometimes forgotten that the depth of lesser-celebrated writing talent in the region is also unusually strong. This anthology highlights that deep base of exceptional writing.

The title of the anthology is taken from the Skyline Drive, the parkway skipping along the top of the Blue Ridge Mountains in Virginia and providing centering for the region in which the authors showcased here are living and writing.

There is no overarching theme for the works in this anthology, so each can be discovered as a fascinating gem of its own luster. Three-quarters of the works found here are works by Central Virginia writers that ranked high in various writing contests during 2013. The foundation is the 2013 writing contest of the Blue Ridge Writers Chapter of the Virginia Writers Club. Added to this is a representative smattering of other works by Central Virginia writers that garnered writing awards in 2013. The remaining fourth of the anthology includes invited "special contributor" works by established writers in the region.

The anthology consists of thirty-four works by twenty-two authors in four sections: fiction, poetry, nonfiction, and, since this is a writer's anthology, a section on writing and publishing. Eclectic is the hallmark word for this collection. The fiction takes the reader from the primeval jungle of "Escape," through the tale of a talking beet of "Herbie the Beet," to a lounge bar singer's pining for lost love in "Playing Nightly." The poetry delves into the personal from the sensuality of "Night Moths" to the musicality and sentimentality of a daughter's wedding in "Lost . . . and Found." The nonfiction moves between the personal experience revealed in the titles of "The

African Queen" and "Emergency Operation" to delving into Central Virginia history via "Taking the Waters" and "The Day Anastasia Ticked Off Rasputin's Daughter." The writing and publishing section is both humorous, as in "Don't Iron Your Clothes While They're on Your Body No Matter How Late You Are," and instructive to developing writers, as in "Feedback: Where to Draw the Line" and "What Counts." Even in this section the deeply personal connection to writing is touched with the literary criticism essay, "A Poem of Impact and Permanence."

Most of the works included have been selected for publication through a juried process. The fiction was judged by North Carolina novelist and poet Joanna Catherine Scott; the poetry by University of Virginia professor of English and creative writing Lisa Russ Spaar and Shenandoah Valley poet and novelist Lori Dixon; and the nonfiction by *Orange County Review* managing editor Jeff Poole.

The varied themes and high quality of writing of the chosen works have made them a delight to work with as volume editor. I'm sure you will be as surprised and pleased as I was, as you work your way from one independently formed gem to the next in this jewel-studded necklace that is *Skyline 2014*.

Olivia Stowe
Volume Editor
Skyline 2014

PROSE FICTION

Escape

Deborah M. Prum

Running, running.

Baying hounds. Angry shouts. Growling and howling from a distance.

He's three, maybe four minutes ahead of the mob who killed his wife and child.

Empty sky except for a blazing sun.

Blood streams down his face, obscuring his vision. Pulse throbbing against his eardrums. His parched mouth is metallic with terror. He smells the stench of his own fear dripping from every pore. Each gasp of breath stabs his lungs. His heart crashes against broken, aching ribs. He hurtles forward on the shredded soles of his naked feet.

The narrow trail ends. A cliff. Sheer drop to one hundred fifty feet below. Roiling water. Razor-edged rocks.

From behind him, roaring and shrieking. Feet pounding down the packed path. Coming closer and closer.

He frantically scans in all directions. He spots a rope. Twisted brown strands, partially unraveling, fastened to a scraggly slip of a slender tree.

His fingers tremble as he ties the frayed cord around his waist. He peers over the edge. Such a long way down. Bowels churn, knees grow spongy with terror.

Men and dogs loom large at the edge of the woods. Shouts of triumph. The prey is trapped.

One brief wordless prayer sent heavenward. Then he flings himself over the cliff. Time slows. The rope grows taut and then jerks the small tree out by its roots.

He falls, falls, falls.

He crashes onto an outcropping of bushes. The rest of the rope and tree fly over his head, both snagging on rocks just below. With all his strength, scraping knees and chest, he hoists himself onto the slimmest of ledges.

He looks down. Maybe a hundred feet? Too steep to descend and too far to jump.

Well above his head, he hears frenzied barking and vituperative curses, the men and dogs cheated by his leap.

He sinks onto the tiny patch of soil and covers his face with his hands, grief wrenching his soul. What's this? A scent of honey? He inhales deeply, breathing in a light fragrance reminiscent of his wife's embrace.

He opens his palms. Purple and blue, stains not bruises. Turning his head, he sees against the rock face, with gnarled roots anchored in the scant soil, two blueberry bushes, laden with fat blue fruit. He picks a perfect dusky orb and slips it into his mouth. Rolling, rolling the berry, finding comfort in the smooth, smooth, skin. Closing his eyes, he nestles into the stone crevice, still warm from the sun.

Then, with his tongue, he crushes the blueberry against the roof of his mouth. Flavor bursts onto his palate, sweet and tart, imbued with all the hope of his son's gentle laugh. He swallows, savoring the nourishment.

He tilts his face upward and allows the setting sun to bless him. Then he reaches for another berry.

The Famous Poet's Umbrella

Jody Hobbs Hesler

(First Place fiction, Writer's Eye contest, 2012, from Jean
Helion's "Still Life with Umbrella," from 1939, viewable at
http://www.virginia.edu/artmuseum/pdf/UVaM-WE12-
images2.pdf)

At the beginning of the semester, the famous poet announced
that he would meet one-on-one with any poet he judged worthy
from within the university community. Henry Glasser—an
astrophysics professor awaiting tenure—had been amazed that
his own work had merited such an honor, until he arrived at the
line of chosen poets, which draped the famous poet's hallway,
then passed the water fountain, and reached as far as the
bathroom doors. Faced with the line, Henry recalculated his
enthusiasm. How could there be so many poets? The smell of
patchouli lingered in the air, and nearly every other poet's shirt
was black. Henry wore the only tie. Everyone rustled papers in
their hands—poems they'd brought. How could there be so
many poems?

The scent of old building mixed with the patchouli. The
floor tiles upon which Henry and the other poets sat were an
earthy swirl of gray and reddish-brown, many squares chipped at
the edges or cracked. The walls' austere smoky-blue paint hadn't
been retouched in years. Henry took his place in the line,
resigned to a long wait. He hoped to share his favorite four
poems during his meeting with the famous poet but wasn't sure
this would be permitted. The honor of the meeting included a
critique of the poets' submitted work, and Henry, never having
shown his work to anyone, didn't know what this meant. He
surveyed the line for signs that anyone else shared his confusion.

One young woman's hair tumbled from a carelessly
dangling barrette. Another leaned toward the person next to her,
saying something with rolling eyes. A young man laughed in an
easy way, broadcasting his comfortable connection to this event.
Everyone in line appeared wise to the world of poetry—jaded,

15

even by the prospect of meeting with the famous poet.

Jaded! The famous poet's lines thrummed the very lining of Henry's soul. Tipping his head upward to admire a starry night brought "stars like dust on midnight sand." Inhaling a spring breeze pulled "fragrant air like silken hair and moistest kisses." All Henry's intimate thoughts came as lines of poetry—his own or someone else's. Still, here among these jaded poets, he was the one who didn't belong.

None of Henry's students appeared in the line. In his department, no one else had heard of the famous poet. At the end of last academic year, Henry had stumbled across the article in the local paper that announced the famous poet's appointment as the university's next writer-in-residence. When he'd shared the news, excitedly, at his department meeting, the poet's name had elicited only the blankest stares.

The line snaked its way toward the suite of offices that included the famous poet's temporary quarters. By the time Henry reached the suite—a sofa, two chairs, a side table crowded with folded papers—his watch read 7:30. He'd been waiting almost two hours. Astrophysics students who would wait so long for an audience with a professor would be the ones having the most trouble with the subject matter. Henry knew this.

Below the side table at Henry's left stood an empty wine bottle. Shredded paper dotted the musty rug there, too. An umbrella leaned against the table, striking Henry at once both with its absolute, unpoetic functionality and its sublime indifference to the hand that curled round its handle, to the fact that it was the famous poet's umbrella.

Stationed at the sofa, Henry watched people leaving the poet's office. Jaded no more, they all left with expressions of amazement, humiliation, even fear. Henry's stomach twinged—he had no way to predict his own outcome. In physics he could predict everything. When Henry's turn came, any illusion of the potential worth of his own poetry had dwindled to nothing. Even the lusterless umbrella seemed more deserving of the famous poet's attention.

A meager, crowded room, the office was an odd choice for housing an esteemed visitor. Heaps of manuscripts and moldering, leather-bound volumes cluttered the desk. The last rays of late-spring sun provided the room's only light, slanting from a transom window high above them, shimmering with dust.

"Henry Glasser?" the poet said. Embarrassment stabbed Henry as he recalled the passionate scrawlings he had given the famous poet to read, which must have amounted to no more than the verbal drivel of an absentminded, socially awkward man—products of Henry's fevered restless nights, flashes of clarity in the middle of conference lectures about how stars exploded to form the very stuff of human life.

"You're a fine poet," the man continued. "Your musings on the pond, I assume it's a pond from your home?"

"Yes," Henry said. "My childhood home."

"It called to mind Hardy's work, don't you think?"

Was calling to mind Thomas Hardy in 2012 good or bad? Did this remark suggest that Henry's poetry was unoriginal? Despite his doubts, Henry's long-standing reverence for Hardy, begun in his tenth-grade year when he'd discovered that poet, made him answer, "Yes, I would like to think so."

The famous poet's eyes sparkled; Henry had answered well. Slowly, Henry realized that his own lines had moved the very poet whose luminous phrases had felt so personal to Henry that they'd seemed wrung from his own most private agonies. When it was time for Henry to leave, he rose on legs that quivered under him like seagrass. Whatever he had been walking into the famous poet's office, he walked out a poet.

Lingering, dumbfounded, in the suite, Henry noticed, again, the leaning umbrella. How could it not know its role in the universe? He set his hand upon it and curled his own fingers round the handle the famous poet had held before him.

Later, Henry would lean it against the side table in his own office, where it would stand as much an umbrella as ever—mute, ordinary, equally oblivious to its connection to famous poets and struggling astrophysicists alike. To Henry, this made it his own unexploded star—containing everything.

Joleen Finds Her Voice

Gary D. Kessler

(First place fiction, Blue Ridge Writers VWC, 2013)

Gill was sitting on the porch, rocking and rubbing the head of that old hound dog of his, as Joleen walked up the stone path from the mailbox at the edge of the muddy road. She had walked slow uphill from the bus stop in the nearest town, at the mouth of a fold back into the Blue Ridge. The suitcase she was lugging, balanced on the other side by her guitar case, was heavy, but she wasn't walking slow because of that weight. She was weighed down by something more serious than that.

She worried that Gill would know it as soon as he saw her—that, like his momma, he could see guilt from miles away—or maybe that he could smell it on her. She'd be in for quite a licking if he did. And that would probably be the least of her worries.

Gill turned a wary eye on her as she approached. Buck, the hound dog, looked up, starting a woof as he did, but seeing that it was his master's woman—and no threat to him in the pecking order around here—he just yawned, lowered his muff to between his splayed legs again, and snorted off into sleep.

"Did'ja bring back enough to leave somethin' after paying for the trip and makin' up for your absence?" Gill asked when Joleen had reached the bottom step of the rickety porch. "You know I tol' you this nonsense would stop if it didn't more than pay for itself."

Joleen sighed, set the suitcase down on the dirt and gravel that passed for a lawn at the fringe of the porch steps, placed the guitar case on top of that, and climbed the steps. She crossed over Gill's foot without him moving it and sank into the other rocker, with a second sigh.

"Here. $500. Hope that's enough," she said as she scrounged around in her purse and came up with an envelope stuffed with fifty-dollar bills. "I done pretty good in Roanoke, honey. Won the talent contest and also . . ."

But she saw that Gill wasn't even listening to her. He had his eyes on the greenbacks as he closed his hand over the proffered money. The bills were still in Joleen's hand when he did that. Gill stood up from the rocker, still holding Joleen's hand in his grip. "Well, let's go into the house then. I want some."

"Oh, Gill," Joleen answered, trying to keep the tired whine out of her voice. "It's afternoon yet. And I've just walked the three miles from town—after the long bus ride from Roanoke—and there's some chores needin' done, I'm sure."

"You been gone five days, Joleen. What 'ja expect I'd want when you got back? Git on in the house now."

Buck raised his head and gave a little growl as Joleen walked past him into the house. Neither greenbacks nor the woman's reappearance in his life impressed him much.

From the minute they entered the house Joleen expected Gill to stop, grab her arm, and snarl, "You been with another man, ain't you?" But it never came. Gill was concentrating hard on getting his own pleasure out of her.

He hadn't even asked her what she'd won the $500 for doing in the talent contest.

The man in Roanoke had been older and uglier than Gill, but at least he'd given her some time and attention.

It wasn't her first beauty pageant—she'd had to win a few to get this far—but it was sort of make-or-break time for her now. There hadn't been too many Miss Virginias older than she would be come November. The state pageant was held down in Roanoke, and it had been hell to pay to get Gill to let her go from out of their southwest Virginia hollow to compete. She was sure that, if the event had been held in Norfolk, he wouldn't have let her go, like he didn't let her go last year when it was in northern Virginia. Roanoke was farther away then he'd ever let her travel before. That's why, when the trip to Nashville came up, she just told him she was going to Roanoke again. He didn't ask why Roanoke again; he'd just snorted that she'd best come back with as much as she did the last time she went there.

He was jealous about how far she went, even though it usually seemed that he cared more for his hound than for her. But she'd shown him the list of prize money, and he'd begrudgingly told her she could try it, although it looked like a lot of foolishness to him. When she'd asked him if he was coming to cheer her on, he just gave her his "Are you from outer space?" look and asked her if she didn't realize how important his job was down at the garage in town.

When Joleen had won the talent contest with her singing and guitar playing, she realized for the first time that she had a shot at the finals. The top woman went straight to the nationals with the Miss Virginia title, and the next two would get to go on to Nashville for a regional Miss South contestant to also go to a national pageant.

She reasoned later that this had probably been her downfall that had led her into sin—the glimmer of a hope for getting farther.

She'd been in the ballroom of the Hotel Roanoke convention center, waiting along with all of the other girls for the construction workers and designers to stop fussing on stage so that they could practice their evening gown walk when she'd heard the page over the loudspeaker.

"Miss Worthington . . . Miss Pulaski, to the reception desk, please." That was her, Joleen. Both of them were her. She was a Worthington. Gill was a Scragg, but, thankfully, she was still a Worthington. But she also was Miss Pulaski. That was her title—the town she represented in the pageant.

When she went to hotel reception, the man behind the desk held out a folded note. "Please meet me in the Starbucks three blocks to the north now," was what was written, but what was important was that it was signed "One who can make a difference."

As soon as she saw him sitting there, drinking his coffee inside the Starbucks, Joleen knew what this was about. It was the head judge of the pageant. Perhaps if this wasn't probably her last-chance year—and more perhaps if she hadn't won the talent contest and wasn't standing at least on the lower step of the finals podium already—and perhaps if her life wasn't just too, too dreary to not try to break out of, Joleen wouldn't have gone to the man's car. But she did. When he pulled up beside a seedy motel, though, Joleen ran out of courage while he was, as he said, getting a "taste of her," and she managed to put him off the hunt—politely, she thought.

"No hard feelings?" she'd asked, hoping he wasn't mad at her.

"Naw, honey. I just wanted to be with a winner. I'm sure you'll win."

What he'd said made Joleen feel real good. Only later did she feel the guilt, and her greatest sin was that she didn't feel the guilt until she had won the second runner-up spot. She was sure that he had promised her the crown.

When she had managed to maneuver him to where only he could hear her whisper and had voiced her pique, he merely smiled and murmured that he'd only said she'd win—not what she'd win—and if she had really wanted the crown, she should have given him what Miss Fairfax had.

Months later she would feel fortunate that she hadn't won the crown—that she'd gone to Nashville next rather than straight to Las Vegas.

When she'd gotten home from Roanoke, there was only one thing on Gill's mind. Even Buck didn't give her a woof; he just lifted his head, gave her a dismissive look, and rolled over for Gill to reach down and rub his belly.

Joleen knew she was second best to Gill's hound. And that Buck didn't care any more than Gill did that she was now the second runner-up to Miss Virginia—or even that she'd come home with another $500 for that matter.

Not for the first time she wondered how she'd feel if Gill asked her to marry him—not that the thought had ever entered his mind, she was sure. But if he did, she knew her world would crumble into nothingness. Whatever she did from this point in her life, she knew her life was going to have to get better. She'd see to that herself. She was the second runner-up to Miss Virginia.

* * * *

Only in Nashville could Joleen have had the revelation.

As soon as she arrived there for the regional pageant, she realized she was badly out of her depth. There was beauty on all sides of her in the dressing rooms. Perfect beauty. Manufactured beauty. Scraped-on beauty. Joleen's was a natural beauty. That no longer cut it in the realm of beauty pageants. What was interesting, intriguing, attracting in her features was a flaw in the eyes of the system at this level.

Reality assaulted her at every turn. She would have been crushed, would have wanted to open her veins and just melted away if . . . if she hadn't won the talent competition in Nashville just as she had in Roanoke.

This meant she could go home to Gill with prize money in hand—more than $1,000 this time. He wouldn't care where it had come from, what part of the competition had provided it. He took her beauty as just his right—his right as the biggest stud in the Pulaski region—his right to claim the county rose and to use her until she was wan and flabby from too many pregnancies and calloused and worn out from a hardscrabble life. That she had a clear-toned mournful soprano voice that could loosen hearts and moisten tear ducts and was matched with a sure stroke of the guitar strings meant nothing to him. He didn't even realize it. As far as Joleen knew, Gill had never stayed around to hear her sing. All he knew or wanted of her was that, by his having her, no other man in Pulaski could.

Being in Nashville, home of country music, and winning the beauty pageant talent contest with her country music songs provided groundwork for the revelation. Billy Ray Furness provided the rest.

Billy Ray was the darling of the regional pageant. He was about the biggest talent producer in Nashville, and the pageant bowed and scraped to him because he was providing the nationally acclaimed country music legends of song as the glue that would hold the regionally televised final night ceremonies of the pageant together.

Where he walked in the halls of the events pavilion, people genuflected. Whatever he wanted, he got.

The evening of the final judging of talent, he got all starry-eyed at Joleen's performance. He made no bones about talking it up in the hearing of the judges and Joleen alike. He said she could be a recording star—that he could make her a star and that wouldn't it be wonderful publicity for the pageant to have

22

the story of a star born on their stage floating around in the national entertainment media?

The selection of Joleen as the winner of that portion of the competition was universal, almost by acclaim. And the applause for her impromptu encore was even more thundering than for her winning performance.

The pageant officials were delighted to provide Billy Ray a very private dressing room backstage when he told them he'd have a proposition to put to Joleen that would launch a major career. The pageant officials were giddy with joy not only on Joleen's behalf but also on behalf of their publicity department.

The proposition Billy Ray had to give to Joleen amid declarations of what a star she would be and how closely they could work together as country singer and mentor business manager only belatedly sank in with Joleen when he closed the door of the very private dressing room. All Joleen could think of was how she had messed up and ended up as a second runner-up and how Billy Ray was pointing to a career that had opened up to her by coming to Nashville rather than straight to Las Vegas—built not on fleeting physical beauty but on her talent as a country singer.

The next morning, Joleen couldn't find Billy Ray anywhere, nor could anyone she talked to tell her how she could contact him. The closest she got to tracking him down was the vague suggestion that he had left that morning for Los Angeles.

Joleen might have returned to the hollow in the folds of the Blue Ridge in despair if it had not been for the revelation. She need not try to make the most of fleeting beauty. Her voice would far outlast that. She was a country singer. Billy Ray had had his little fun, but the applause in that large auditorium was real. And it had made love to her in ways and to depths no man had.

When she arrived at the mailbox on the verge of the muddy road in a taxi, Gill just stood up from his rocker and waited for her to climb the front porch stairs. Buck gave her the usual woof of derision, and Gill closed his hand over the one Joleen proffered her contest win prize money in and led her into the farmhouse.

* * * *

Unsurprisingly, Gill hadn't asked what Joleen had won to be bringing home a good chunk of money—or why she'd driven up in a taxi rather than walking home from the bus station—and, most interesting of all, why she said she had another beauty pageant to go to in Richmond that might last two weeks. She brought money home; and as long as she did that and followed him into the farmhouse when she came back, that was enough for Gill. He had enough to worry about down at the garage. He didn't have time to check on whether or not there was a beauty pageant on in Richmond.

Gill was so taken with trying to figure out what was going amiss with the transmission on the mayor's Cadillac that he didn't even notice that when Joleen left for Richmond, she packed three bags, rather than the one—enough to hold all of her clothes and her momma's silver—and left in a taxi. Buck noticed, though. He stood on the porch and wagged his tail while Joleen hauled the bags and guitar case out to the taxi in two loads—right under Gill's nose. If it could be said a dog smiled, Buck was smiling. Joleen always did say that Buck had more brains than Gill did.

She had made all of the arrangements in Richmond beforehand. A recording studio and an experienced sound technician, a nice young guy named Paul. Joleen thought he had a great smile. And he was ultrapolite, yes ma'ming her left and right and being real attentive to all of her requests as she sat there, in the recording booth, for hours, and sang her haunting laments, all her own creations—all the flowing forth of short, but hard, years of trials and tribulations.

After they were done, Joleen just sat there, exhausted, in the silence. No applause, no nothing. She stood up from the stool and walked into the sound booth. Paul was sitting there, looking down at his controls.

"Well?" she asked, not sure she wanted to hear his reaction.

He looked up, and quietly said, "Wow. Just wow."

Joleen wondered what he meant, though. He was looking vaguely at the level of her tits. But if he thought he was going to

24

get anything, he was sadly mistaken. She'd paid him in cash for his time. She was a little irritated. Is that what they all are thinking of, she wondered. He had seemed to be a nice guy.

"What are you going to do with this recording?" he asked.

"Start trying to sell it around, I guess," she answered. She knew it wasn't going to be easy, though. She knew after a couple of weeks she'd have to find some work. She sure as hell knew she wasn't going back to Pulaski and Gill.

"OK if I see if I can get them someplace?" he asked.

"Sure, why not?" she answered.

A week later, Paul called her at her motel and said he might have a proposition for her. Could she meet him at the West End Starbucks on Broad? It was near her motel; she knew he knew it was near her motel.

Here we go again, she thought. But nothing had panned out in Richmond yet. She'd found Billy Ray's address in Nashville and sent the recording off there—as well to other music producers in Nashville—but she'd heard nothing back.

So, OK, if this Paul has a better lead than she had developed so far, yes, she'd give him what he wanted. But he'd better have more than just empty promises. She'd been too far down that road already. It was time for her to be the one using and taking advantage of someone else.

Paul was looking real good when she showed up at Starbucks. He was nattily dressed—all groomed, like he wanted them to video the results of his proposition. If he got lucky.

"You're late," he said. He looked almost panicked about that. "I was afraid you wouldn't come."

"I almost didn't," Joleen said. "I've been around this proposition in Starbucks deal once too often."

"Shush," he said.

"Shush what? Why?" Joleen answered, a little piqued.

"Just shush and listen. Sit down and listen. Listen to the music."

Joleen sat. And Joleen began to listen. And Joleen realized she was listening to Joleen—coming from the radio. One of her own songs, sung by her. And then, after that ended, she heard another of her songs, again sung by her. Coming over the speakers on the radio.

She was trembling, her palm on top of Paul's on the table top. She felt him tremble too, enjoying the experience as much as she was—and not just the experience of hearing herself on the radio.

"You got my songs on the radio here in Richmond?" she asked.

"Yeah. I've got a few connections. They ate them right up. And not just here in Richmond. This is a syndicated show. This is going out all over the south."

Joleen's cell phone was buzzing. A text message. Billy Ray Furness. "Where did u go? We were going to talk contract. Call me," it said. Joleen flipped the phone off. She'd see what he had to offer later, but he wasn't high on her list at the moment.

Paul had done this for her. No strings attached. He'd just gone ahead and done it. Hadn't demanded or asked anything from her.

"That was a Nashville record producer," she said. "Already talking recording contract."

"That's good. But go slow. There will be others."

"You'll help me?"

"If you want. Any way you want."

They paused, frozen in place, Joleen's hand on Paul's again. They were both looking at the hands, as if they probably should let loose, but neither wanted to.

"Should we celebrate? Go someplace and celebrate?" Joleen murmured.

"If you like," Paul said.

"My motel room OK?" Joleen asked. She was already thinking ahead. She knew he'd be good and attentive.

"Maybe we should go slow on that too," Paul said.

"You don't want . . . ?"

"Sure I do. Of course I do. But you should be sure and shouldn't, you know, go there because of any of this. You have more hours at the studio. Do you have any more sad songs in you?"

"You bet, I do." And then she smiled. "And I see some happier songs boiling up inside me too."

Back on the porch of the farmhouse outside of Pulaski, Gill was sitting and rocking, thinking somewhere in the back of his mind, somewhere in back of reviewing the brake relining job he had to do in the morning, that it should be about time for Joleen to be coming home from that fool pageant in Richmond. She'd better have some good cash in hand, was all he thought.

He stirred, hearing the sound of the radio cutting through his other thoughts. Some woman was singing a sad song on the radio. The voice sounded sort of familiar and the song was real pretty. But he couldn't quite place who was doing the singing.

At his side, flattened out on the worn wood of the porch, Buck, recognizing the voice instantly, put his paws over his ears, and emitted a low moan.

Herbie the Beet

Leonard Tuchyner

(Second place fiction, Blue Ridge Writers VWC, 2013)

It was one of those oh-so-rare days in late spring when nature conspires to bring all of her most wondrous attributes together to make a fanatic gardener leap for joy at the prospect of spending a morning in the vegetable garden pulling weeds. A solid day of downpour three days previously had been followed by a time of dry, overcast weather in which sodden soil morphed gently into loamy clay. One afternoon of Central Virginia sun had dried the soil's surface so that here I was, the following morning, on hands and knees, perched on ground that did not cleave muddily to clothes and skin. Yet the weeds, which had had aspirations of conquest, were vanquished easily from a moist, crumbly soil resting just below the surface. A balmy breeze gently cooled and warmed as it caressed the back of my neck and shoulders.

The air was alive with the symphony of bird sounds sung by permanent residents and migrants returning from winter vacations. Canadian geese barked on the lake, a catbird squawk-mewed, a cardinal sang, "Pretty, pretty, pretty," and a mourning dove cooed its mystery moan.

Suddenly, a small, childlike voice shocked me into attention. "Ah, excuse me."

"What? Who said that?" I almost strained my neck searching for the speaker.

"It's me . . . down here."

My brain would not accept what my ears were telling me. The little voice came from below. It was a little softer and further away, because somehow I had bolted to my feet.

"Who?"

"Me."

I stared down at the row of beets I had been weeding, looking for . . . for what? Then I smiled and burst out laughing.

"OK, you got me. I've got to admit, you sure had me going. So where did you get the remote speaker?"

I began to probe the ground for signs of a minispeaker that someone obviously must have buried there, watching unseen for me to get close enough.

"What are you doing?" the little voice asked.

"Am I on *Candid Camera*?"

"What's a candid camera?" it asked.

My jocularity faded and my smile turned downward as my probing became almost desperate.

"OK, enough's enough. It's not funny anymore. Come on out, wherever you're hiding. Maybe there is no buried speaker. Maybe your voice is being projected somehow. But I'm getting scared and mad. Cut it out."

"Are you talking to me?" the little voice asked, confusion in its tone.

Sherlock Holmes once said something like, "When you have exhausted all possible explanations, there remains only the impossible."

My eyes searched the location of the voice, and my own voice became as quiet and childlike as the bodiless one that tormented me. "What are you?"

"I'm just a little beet sprout. But you must know that."

"Which one?"

"I'm the tallest, widest, reddest one in the row," it said with obvious pride.

A beet of that description lay just below me. I dropped to my knees and examined it.

"Why are you talking?"

"Why shouldn't I talk?"

"I never heard of a talking beet. You don't hear any other beets talking, do you now?"

"That's true. They won't say a word. I've begged them to say something to me, but they just turn a deaf ear."

"That must be very frustrating."

"You have no idea. It's very lonely. It's being lonely in a crowd."

I knelt there in silence, not knowing where next to bring the conversation. The silence was awkward, neither one of us knowing what to say.

Finally, "What's your name?"

"Well, nobody ever gave me a name, so I named myself. I'm Herbert."

"Uh, nice to meet you, Herbie."

Well, for the next couple of weeks, Herbert and I got to be good friends. He was actually a good conversationalist and very helpful. For example, one day, as I was working at the far end of the garden, I heard Herbie calling to me. I noticed his voice was changing. It was getting lower, and every once in a while it had a crack in it. I reasoned he was getting to be a teenager, and in only a couple of weeks. How about that?

"Leonard, Leonard." he called. That's because my name is Leonard.

"I'll be right there, Herbie."

I finished hoeing the potato row and then headed for the beet section.

"What is it, Herbie?" I looked around, as I always did. I didn't want any of the neighbors to catch me talking to a beet. It's not that the neighbors are particularly prejudiced against beets. Oh, I admit that some of them don't like the chubby little red fellows, but that's because they weren't brought up with them.

"Leonard, I'm very grateful for all the time you've put into keeping me healthy and satisfied, but I do have something on my mind."

"I'm listening."

"I just don't want to seem ungrateful, Leonard."

"Don't think twice, it's all right."

"Well, it's just that you're hoeing a little too close. It makes me nervous."

"I don't think so. It's important to get all the weeds I can," I said, a little defensively.

"You cut off a feeder root the last time, and I notice you're hoeing the garden today."

"Oh? I'm sorry. I'll have to be more careful," I admitted begrudgingly.

"And as long as we're talking about your gardening prowess, you are overwatering a bit. That isn't good for a clay soil."

I felt like telling the green and red guy that it was none of his business and to do it himself if he thought he could do better. But then I realized that it *was* his business and he couldn't water himself, even if he wanted to. Besides, I guess I wouldn't want my feeder roots cut, if I had feeder roots or any kind of roots at all, for that matter.

"OK, Herbert, I'll be more careful and water a little less."

After that, Herbie gave me all kinds of advice. Some of it was hard to hear. But, hey, he was making me a better gardener. How many people do you know who have a talking beet to guide them, or any talking vegetable, for that matter?

About a week later, when Herbie had an actually noticeable bulb developing, we were having a conversation about rabbits, when suddenly, out of the blue, he asked, "Are you God?"

I'd been gazing at a puffy white cloud at the time, but my head jerked around to stare at Herbie, in astonishment. "Wha . . . ? why do you ask something like that?"

"Well, here I am, sitting almost in the middle of this wonderful garden. Oh, I know that little bit of sleet we got last week wasn't so wonderful, but all in all, it's pretty grand. The rows are straight, more or less. We're arranged side by side. The other plants are also set up in well-ordered patterns. So I wonder can this order be an accident? What are the chances of seeds landing in a nonrandom arrangement? It certainly smacks of an intelligent design. It has to be somebody's plan. I think it was you. So you must be God."

I stared at the beet in astonishment. "Herbie, if I were God, wouldn't I have had to create your seed to begin with?"

"Hmmmm." And with that, Herbie stayed silent, deep in thought, for the rest of the day.

The next day, it was drizzling, but I was so anxious to see if Herbie was OK that I went into the garden anyway.

"Herbie, are you all right?"

"I'm not sure. How did I get here, Leonard?"

For the next couple of hours, I taught Herbie about the birds and the bees.

"Leonard, are you God?" There was a plaintive demanding sound in his voice.

Not only did I have a talking beet on my hands, but I had a metaphysical philosopher to boot.

"If I am, Herbie, so are you."

"How is that possible?"

"Look, Herbie, you're in this garden with a whole lot of beets, some peas, potato plants, bean plants, and weeds. Are you a beet, or are you the garden?"

"I'm a beet."

"You're a freaking miracle, but let me ask you this. Would it be a garden without all the plants and weeds?"

If Herbie had eyes, they would have almost popped out of his head—if he had a head. After a while . . .

"No. It wouldn't be a garden. It would just be a bunch of dirt with a fence around it."

"Actually, Herbie, it would be a potential garden. But no matter, you get my point."

"But I can't be a garden all by myself. I'm only part of the garden."

"Right."

"Am I part of God?"

"That's my belief, Son."

"What's going to happen to me, Leonard?"

Now, that question really shook me up. That's why I pretended not to know where this questioning was destined to lead us.

"I suspect you'll grow into a big, healthy, dark-red ball, with beautiful red and green plumage."

"Then what?"

"You'll make your seed, and little Herbies and Herbellas will grow in the garden next year. I'll see to it."

"There isn't enough room in the garden for my seed and the seed of all my fellow beets. What's going to happen to them?"

I had been dreading this question. I had hoped that Herbie wouldn't have figured things out that well. But he is the smartest beet I ever met.

"Herbie, it's difficult for me to talk to you about this. But vegetables are grown in gardens to be eaten or to produce seed."

"Eaten?!"

"It's not the way it sounds" I said, though I knew it was exactly the way it sounded.

"Eaten like that rabbit ate that turnip green last week, Leonard?"

"Yeah."

"I'm scared. What happens to me even if you don't eat me?"

I felt like a doctor telling his best friend that he had terminal cancer. "You'll grow old and woody. All your leaves will dry up, and you'll rot in the ground."

I felt Herbie looking at me and wanted to crawl away into the ground like a mole.

"Thanks for giving it to me straight, Leonard. I guess you're not really God. I know you wouldn't allow that to happen to me, if you were."

"Look, Herbie, I don't really understand this, but you know God doesn't die. If we're all parts of God, then we don't die either. The same fate that awaits you is in store for me. It will only take longer. Somehow I'll still be around, just not exactly the same."

"You don't really know, Leonard, do you?"

"No."

"Will you let any of my fellow beets go to seed?"

"I will if you want me to, Herbie."

"But that's not what you had planned to do, is it?"

"No."

"I don't want to go to seed, Leonard."

"Oh . . . ?"

"I want to be eaten by you. I want to reach my potential. Do my job. Then I want to be picked at my largest, yet most tender and nutritious point. Finally, I want to fulfill the last stage

33

of my destiny by nurturing the one who nurtured me. Maybe that way I'll be a part of you and you'll be part of me."

I was speechless. Tears ran down my face. Although I never thought I would be part of a beet, they do say that we are what we eat. We stayed there, still and quiet, for a long time.

"Herbie."

"Yes, Leonard?"

"When the time comes, you let me know."

"I don't want to decide such a thing all by myself. I want you to help me."

"OK."

* * * *

In midsummer, there came a time when Herbie was showing signs of going to seed. I tried to deny that he was past his nutritional prime. But I had promised to help him know when the time had come.

"Herbie, if you don't want to go to seed, it has to be today. You can change your mind, you know."

"I can't. I won't. I know I'm already getting pithy in the middle. Will it hurt, Leonard?"

"I don't think so. Maybe for a moment, when your roots are pulled up. But then your leaves will simply dry out and you'll stop producing chlorophyll. I think it will be peaceful and gradual. But Herbie, I don't really know. No beet that I've ever heard of was able to talk about it."

"Go ahead and do it now. Then lay me in the sun and stay with me, Leonard."

"Of course, old friend."

I pulled him out right there and then before he had a chance to worry about it, and before I lost my nerve.

"That wasn't so bad," he said in a weakening voice. "I can feel myself fading. I kind of feel like I do when I haven't been watered for a long time. It's kind of peaceful."

"You told me I was overwatering you."

"You never got the balance just right."

"I'm sorry."

"You did the best you could. You're only human."

34

"Yeah. Look, Herbie, I could put you in a bowl of water. You'd stay perky for a while."

"No. This is the right time and the right way. No drastic life support systems for me."

I sat with him most of the day, until I was sure he was gone. Needless to say, I was full of tears and doubts. In his last moments, he said he felt he was floating away and that death was not death. He said "Good-bye," and was gone.

That night I celebrated Herbie's life by making him the center of a boiled-beet salad. He was truly food for the gods.

* * * *

I plant beets every spring these days. I keep listening very closely, because I know, someday, I'm going to hear a child's voice in the beet rows saying, "Ah, excuse me."

Caroline's Essential Emporium

Justin Fike

(Third place fiction, Blue Ridge Writers VWC, 2013)

There is no magic in the world. Nothing I've seen in the past fifty years has changed my mind on that account. While she was with me I started to believe otherwise, but I think Caroline just had that effect on folks. Now I'm closing up her shop for the last time.

Wisehaupt's the name, and it suits. "Old and proud," she always said, but she never took it herself. "There is no magic in Wisehaupts, darling." I never blamed her, though. Caroline LeFey did carry a certain kind of sparkle.

The sign above the door reads Caroline's Essential Emporium. I think the name is the only reason folks ever nosed her place out. Wasn't the easiest to find. It sits halfway down the block on Constance, in the first floor of what used to be a candle shop. The smell of dry wax fills up my dreams sometimes. It's cluttered and jumbled; shelves and mismatched tables piled high with all the odd little things Caroline drew to herself. Ceramics, old vinyls, velvet paintings, and rusted iron locks the size of dinner plates, her treasures seemed to appear overnight to fill the spaces left behind when one of her rare customers left with exactly what they hadn't known they'd needed until they walked through the door. The shop's sign is faded and chipped, just like everything else on Constance. It has the look of something that's been touched for luck a few too many times.

The tarnished brass key is warm in the palm of my hand, and as I turn it in the lock for the last time, I can't help but wonder why in the hell she put her shop way back here. "Doesn't make the least bit of sense," I told her years ago. Two blocks over from Constance is Park Avenue. You can buy anything you want and two things you don't on Park. The only reason anyone ever wandered back this way is if they already knew the shop was here, or perhaps if they simply knew that they didn't want to be there.

"Excuse me, sir?" pipes a mouse voice behind me. I turn to see a little brown thing standing there, all curls and overlarge shoes. I raise her an eyebrow.

"Is Caroline in, please?" she asks, hooking a thumb toward the silent shop.

"No."

"Well . . . could you tell me when she'll be back, please?"

She walks right up to me, until she has to tilt her head back to look me in the eye. She has big eyes that fill her face, green and quick and curious. They're framed by a swirl of freckles. My heart jumps up and punches me in the throat. Caroline had those freckles. I told her once that I thought they looked like the stars at night. She kissed me with a smile and started to cry.

"She won't," I say, shaking my head to clear it. "She's dead."

Her face just caves in. "Oh . . . oh dear, that's just . . . just awful," she squeaks, her eyes blinking butterfly fast.

"But she can't be! I owe her this," she protests, as she begins rooting in a weathered knapsack I hadn't seen hiding on her back, hidden beneath the curls. She pulls out a small wooden box, simple but very beautiful. It pulls at me, but I keep my hands still at my side.

"I came here to the shop a few months back. I hadn't seen my mom in a few years. She and my dad . . . well, you know, and so I live with my dad now here in the city. I hadn't seen her in a while, but I was supposed to go stay with her over the summer, and I thought if I could bring her just the right present to say 'hi,' then she'd know I wasn't angry . . . well, not too angry anyway . . . and we'd be OK, you know?"

I mumble something agreeable because I think she expects an answer, but she is looking down at her too-large shoes as she spills out her story, and I don't think she even hears me.

"So I was over shopping on Park, but, man, everything over there is so expensive and shiny and none of it was *right* . . . you know? But then I found this place and I told Caroline all about my mom and everything. She said she had just the thing, and boy was she right, 'cause mom loved it! We sat in the

37

kitchen eating pumpkin bread and talked about school and stuff all day."

She finally looks up at me again, and I wonder how something so small can carry such weight in her eyes.

"But Caroline wouldn't let me pay her for it! She just said that if everything worked out then I should bring her back something I loved as a trade, and that . . . wait . . . what's your name?"

"Henry."

"Oh!" she squeaks, "that's great! She said Henry would be here today and that he . . . or, you, I guess . . . would need it."

She stands as if she really is waiting for an answer this time, but I don't know what to say to that one.

"Soooo, I guess this is yours then, Henry," she says and gently deposits the box in my hands.

"I have to get back home now, but um, thanks. Bye, Henry!"

I watch as she turns and half-runs back up the block the way she came. As she reaches the corner, she stops and looks back over her shoulder. The setting sun burns through the gaps in her curls, and I can't see her face anymore.

"She really loved you, you know!" she shouts back at me, and then she is gone.

I stand still for a long time. No one else wanders by, so her parting words float undisturbed in the air around me. Finally, I look down at the box in my hands. The dark brown wood grain swims like fresh coffee. The lid is held down by a small brass clasp that glows in the sun like something that has been touched for luck a few too many times. I flip back the clasp and open the lid, and the delicate gears that had been waiting inside begin playing our song.

I stand there for a long time, listening. That song is a memory I don't care to share with you. When it runs itself out I close the lid, take the key out of my pocket, climb up the familiar steps, and unlock the shop's front door.

There is no magic in the world. Nothing I've seen in the past fifty years has changed my mind on that account. But there was Caroline, and I think that's enough for me.

Meeting the Enemy

Phyllis Anne Duncan

"We have met the enemy, and he is us."

Pogo by Walt Kelly

"Damn it," Mai Fisher cursed after the knock on the door woke her. She dragged herself up to sit on the edge of her cot.

"Come," she called out.

Chin, the math genius with an affinity for the myriad languages of the Middle East, opened the door and stuck in his head. With a smiled apology, he said, "Sorry to wake you, Boss. Max called. He and a visitor will be here at 0900 local."

She glanced at her watch. Less than two hours from now. "What kind of visitor?" she asked, stifling a yawn.

"He didn't say. Sounded official, though. You want us to clean up The Sheik?"

"No, but since I'm awake now, wake him and set him up in main interrogation. Make sure he stays awake."

"Sure thing, Boss." Chin's head disappeared, and the door started to close.

"And how many times have I asked you not to call me boss?"

"Oh, about a thousand, Boss." She heard his chuckle before the door shut.

Forcing herself alert, Mai glanced around the dingy room and sighed. The damp chill that crept from the concrete floor through her socks reminded her of the old houses where she'd grown up in England, ones where her ancestors had eschewed central heating.

Not that she'd expected much comfort while in charge of a CIA rendition center in an old Romanian secret police prison. She had hoped for some decent sleep after her most recent bout with her prisoner. Her only prisoner, not the prisoner she wanted, but an important one.

The muscles in her back protested when she stood. She ran a hand through her dark hair and switched on the lamp atop the crate that served as her nightstand. Giving in to the yawn, she began to dress.

* * * *

Max and his visitor arrived on time, and Chin showed them to Mai's makeshift office. Somewhere in the prison they'd scraped up two sturdy chairs and arranged them across from Mai's "desk"—a door across two columns of bricks.

Max let his companion enter first. A thirtyish, salon blonde, she'd pulled her long hair back in a ponytail and looked as if she'd stopped in Eddie Bauer's before making this trip. Good, sturdy hiking boots—shine undimmed; khaki cargo pants; a cream-colored, cashmere turtleneck over which she wore a brown, sleeveless fleece vest. She had diamond studs—at least a half carat each—in her ears, a double strand of pearls over the turtleneck, and an expensive, leather briefcase. A woman's Rolex and a large gold wedding ring studded with diamonds completed the outfit.

Mai almost laughed. Good thing this woman had Max with her. In Bucharest, some Balkan *Mafiya* would have left her naked and bleeding in an alley within an hour of her arrival.

"Mai," Max said in greeting.

The woman looked around at the squalor, and Mai saw the patrician features twist as if she'd smelled something bad.

"This is—" Max began.

"I'm Sandra Ashton-Jeffrey," the woman said. From a vest pocket she took a small, leather portfolio and flipped it open to reveal a government identification card. She held it for Mai to see. "From the Department of Justice," she said. After several seconds when Mai made no move to take it for examination, she returned it to her pocket. Several more seconds passed as Max rocked on his heels and Mai stared. Ashton-Jeffrey spoke again. "I'm part of the Interrogation Protocols Division."

"There's an Interrogation Protocols Division?" Mai asked.

"Well, right now, it's just me, but I have plans."

I'm sure you do, Mai thought.

"This is Maitland 'Mai' Fisher," Max said. "Operational chief of this facility."

The DOJ woman gave Mai a once-over, and her curled lip showed she wasn't impressed.

"Have a seat, Ms. Jeffrey," Mai said.

"Ashton-Jeffrey." The woman brushed her fingertips across the seat of the chair and examined them; then, she sat, settling her eyes on Mai. "And it's *Mrs.* Ashton-Jeffrey."

Mai cut Max a look, and he rolled his eyes. Mai sat behind her desk. "Very well, to what do I owe the honor of a visit from a DOJ lawyer?"

Ashton-Jeffrey blinked. "How did you know I'm a lawyer?"

"Well, I didn't until you just confirmed it."

Mai got a smile you needed a magnifying glass to see. "Yes, well, all these little spy tricks are something I'm getting accustomed to," Ashton-Jeffrey said. She brought her briefcase to her lap and extracted a piece of paper. "This is for you."

Mai took it and skimmed, noting it was the original of the torture guidelines a White House mole had bootlegged for her some weeks before. Mai put the paper face down on the desk and looked at Ashton-Jeffrey. "Yes?"

"I'd like to explain each of these techniques, so you—"

"I'm aware of them."

Ashton-Jeffrey smiled, her eyes glittering with excitement. "Really? You've used these techniques? How fabulous is that?"

"You misunderstood me. I've been on the receiving end."

"Well, of course. You've been trained in survival, evasion, resistance, and escape, so you—"

"No. I've experienced them at the hands of the KGB and the Stasi."

Ashton-Jeffrey blinked as if she'd just been asked to explain general relativity.

"Old Soviet state security and the former East German secret police," Max said.

He got a look from Ashton-Jeffrey that implied he'd dared to speak without permission. She turned back to Mai. "I need to confirm you are using these techniques on . . ." She paused, glanced around, then lowered her voice, ". . . the prisoner code-named The Sheik."

Mai looked at Max, who nodded. "I have used standard interrogation techniques as described in the U.S. Army Field Manual and CIA protocols—lying, psyops, reward and punishment, and other psychologically coercive methods," Mai said.

Ashton-Jeffrey's mouth opened in astonishment, giving Mai a glimpse of perfect, bright, white teeth. "Reward! You've rewarded a mass murderer?"

"For cooperation and specific information, I've allowed him to have one blanket, which I can take away if he's not cooperating. On occasion, he gets solid food or time without being sensory deprived. This reinforces the behaviors I expect and makes him more forthcoming," Mai said. "All solid, proven, interrogation techniques, which have yielded significant information. Did Max show you my reports?"

"I have seen those reports, and, frankly, that's why I'm here. We think you can elicit additional information from him using more coercive techniques. Like the ones described in the memo."

They could have sent someone who knew what he or she was walking about, but, no, she got an amateur.

"Do you know torture doesn't work?" Mai asked.

"Excuse me?"

"Torture—and the techniques in your memo are just that—doesn't work. Torture only results in the subject's telling you what you want to hear."

This Ashton-Jeffrey smile was the epitome of smug. "Precisely."

"No, people will make things up to get the pain to stop or to have the threat removed."

"Our experts don't agree."

"Who are your experts?"

"Well, that's classified, of course."

"Look, Mrs. Ashton-Jeffrey, real experts call the information received from torture 'white noise.' Static, if you will," Mai said. "It sends us on wild goose chases."

"Rather like what I feel I'm on right now."

Mai smiled. "Let me help you see the difference. When you torture someone, he or she gives up something that sounds credible, just to get whatever you're doing to stop. 'Yes, yes, I saw Bin Laden in Peshawar, living in the house of Mullah Faisal. Now, please stop.' So, while we expend time and assets trying to confirm the information, the prisoner rests up, recovers, and ultimately can resist longer."

"And?"

"And I haven't let up on The Sheik once in the weeks he's been here. I've interrogated him every day, sometimes twenty-four hours a day in shifts. But not once have I tortured him."

"Don't you think it's about time?"

"No."

"What? Why not?"

"My methods are working."

"To a limited degree."

Mai let the first hint of emotion show in the clipped tone in which she replied, "If you understood what you read in my reports, you'd know how I got information out of him."

"Did you promise him a nice, comfy blanket?"

Mai almost laughed. That was sarcasm of her own caliber. "I told him I have his children here, and that if he doesn't tell me what I need to know, I'll start cutting pieces off them."

Ashton-Jeffrey paled beneath the layer of expensive makeup. Her voice shook a little when she said, "The, uh, enhanced techniques will gain more valuable information."

"What more do you want?" Mai asked. "He's taken responsibility for just about every major and minor al Qaeda-related terrorist event since the World Trade Center bombing in 1993 from America to Mombasa. Oh, and that journalist's murder. There's plenty more, all of which we've verified."

"Yes, yes, but that's all in the past," Ashton-Jeffrey said. "We don't care about that."

"You're a lawyer. You know those are confessions admissible even in a military tribunal and enough to convict."

43

"America needs to know where the next attack is coming from. That's far more useful than 'confessions.'"

"You really don't know how this works, do you?"

"What do you mean?"

"We caught him eighteen months after 9/11, and when we did get him, your administration announced it to the world. Communications networks, travel plans, tactical plans, passwords, schedules—all now altered or abandoned. This doesn't work like James Bond or Jack Bauer."

A finger pointed at Mai, Ashton-Jeffrey leaned forward. "I'm ordering you to water board the son of a bitch and find out where the next attack is coming from."

"I don't take orders from you, and if you'd listen, you'd realize he doesn't have a clue now where the next attack is coming from."

"You will water board him."

"I won't break the law and have the evidence I've already collected invalidated," Mai said.

"The memo, if you'd bother to read it, explains that water boarding is legal."

"I know how that memo got signed, and I doubt its legitimacy, much as I doubt yours."

"That memo is signed by a deputy attorney general—"

"Who is a political flunky and signed it because the attorney general wouldn't, even in hospital and under the influence of anesthetic."

"You don't know that. There's no way you can know that," Ashton-Jeffrey said.

"Oh," Max chimed in, "we know that."

The look Ashton-Jeffrey gave Max made Mai expect to see the skin on his face slough to the floor. Then she looked at Mai. "This is your last chance. Water board him."

Mai relaxed in her chair, though she had to keep her temper on a tight rein. "If I were to do that, The Sheik will no longer cooperate, and everything he tells us will be suspect."

"I don't care how cooperative he has been. For what he did, he deserves the harshest punishment we can give him."

"Punishment is the court's purview, not mine. Or yours."

"Semantics. I want him water boarded."

Mai smiled. "I'll tell you what, Mrs. Ashton-Jeffrey, let me water board you, and then you can decide if I should use it on The Sheik."

"What? Are you insane?" Ashton-Jeffrey looked at Max. "Is she crazy?"

"Like a fox," Max replied.

"I'm not the one ordering the torture of a human being," Mai said.

"Human being? How naïve you are, Miss Fisher. He's scum. He's an animal."

"It's Ms. Fisher, by the way, and, right now, I consider him more human than you. Get out of my prison."

"You don't give me orders, either. The president wants The Sheik water boarded in the interest of national security. You will follow the president's order."

"If you want him water boarded, I'll set it up for you. You can have a go."

"Honestly! I don't understand why you can't do as I say!"

"I'll speak slower. I. Don't. Work. For. You."

Ashton-Jeffrey looked at Max. "Order her to do it."

"She doesn't work for me, either," Max said.

In a near whine, Ashton-Jeffrey said, "She has to work for someone."

"I report only to the CIA director," Mai said.

"Well, he works for the president."

"I think you'll find I have a somewhat privileged status in the CIA."

"I really don't understand your issue. It's only water."

"Do you swim?" Mai asked.

"Of course. What's that—"

"Have you ever almost drowned?"

"No, but what—"

"Too bad. It's an apt analogy. In water boarding, you try to swallow the water, but it comes too fast. You think you'll hold your breath, except your torturers won't let you. They'll do something to make you scream, so more water gets in. You're

45

tied down. You can't see, and the water is unending. If we do that to The Sheik, he'll confess he was on the Grassy Knoll."

Mai saw the woman's lower lip quiver.

"You're making all that up," Ashton-Jeffrey said, in a voice so quiet Mai had to strain to hear.

"No. I experienced it."

"You're making that up, too."

"If I'm making it up," Mai said, "again, why don't I just demonstrate on you?"

"You wouldn't dare."

"You think it's no big deal, so what's the problem with a practical demonstration?"

"It's ille . . ." Ashton-Jeffrey clamped her mouth closed.

"Illegal?" Mai finished, another smile in place. "I believe your memo protects me from prosecution. You people turn my stomach. You're all war bluster and 'bring it on,' but none of you has fought a war. You sit around with a bunch of washed-up, military rejects and brainstorm about torture techniques you've seen in television shows and movies. And you know what? If the American people can't see through that, then they deserve the village idiot in the White House."

Max cleared his throat, and Mai caught his head shake. So, she'd gone too far. Not the first time. Not the last. It did, however, bring some defiance back into Ashton-Jeffrey.

"The president, the vice president, are true Americans," she said, her chin lifted. "I'm proud to serve them. Everyone should be."

"Another reason I'm glad I'm not an American," Mai said.

Again, Ashton-Jeffrey turned to Max. "She's not an American?"

"I thought the British accent made it pretty obvious," Max said.

"How can a foreigner work for the top covert organization in the country?"

"There are waivers," Mai said, "for those of us with special skills." Mai looked at Max. "Are we done here? I have a prisoner to interrogate."

Max opened his mouth, but Ashton-Jeffrey spoke. "You will water board him. Starting now."

Mai took a deep breath for calm. "No."

"So, if your child were kidnapped, and the only way to save him was to torture one of his kidnappers, you wouldn't do it?"

Mai laughed and shook her head. "No. Bribe him with a ridiculous amount of money, yes. Better yet, I'd find his family and use them against him. Max, I think my conversation with this Stepford Wife is over. Get her out of my sight."

Max stood. "Let's go, Sandy."

Ashton-Jeffrey crossed her arms again and remained firm in her chair. "I'm here on the authority of the Department of Justice. I'm not leaving until The Sheik is water boarded."

"I won't use a procedure that will garner no credible intelligence and will cast a question on the information I have obtained," Mai said. "If you won't dirty your manicure with it, I'm not your lackey. Find someone else."

Ashton-Jeffrey's smirk returned. "That can be arranged."

* * * *

Though she hated this concession to religious zeal, Mai arranged a *keffiyeh* to cover her hair before she went into the cell with her prisoner. As usual, his eyes flicked to her and away, and he turned a little in his chair so they would not be face to face. She placed her chair closer to him than she normally would, but she wanted only him to hear what she had to say. He sensed that nearness and pressed himself against the back of his chair as far as he could. She knew it wasn't from fear, but from distaste.

"We're not being recorded," Mai told him.

His bearded face, thin from the mostly liquid diet she'd had him on, turned to her. No distaste now. He was skeptical.

"I have things to say," Mai continued, "I don't want on the record. I don't want you to misunderstand why I'm going to tell you this. I know what you are. You're a murdering bastard who uses religion to justify the killing of innocent people. You slaughtered that journalist like an animal."

47

When he opened his mouth to speak, Mai leaned toward him. "No! I'm talking. You don't speak until I let you."

He clamped his mouth closed and looked away from her again.

"But," she said, "it's my personal belief you shouldn't be treated the way you treated that man." His eyes slid to her, lids narrowed. Mai continued, "I've fucked with your head, yes; you tried to fuck with mine, but I've never shed a drop of your blood. You know that."

He gave a single nod in concession.

"I'm leaving, and shortly after, people will come to take you to the detention center in Guantanamo Bay, Cuba. They won't be as considerate as I. They plan to torture you. I want you to understand that and be prepared."

He turned in the chair until he faced her. "Why do you tell me this?"

"I have my reasons."

"Why should I trust what you say? This is another of your mind tricks."

"No. This is no trick."

"Then, why?"

"I said, I have my reasons. That's all you need to know."

She watched as he considered, but his eyes stayed suspicious. Then, he looked away again. "May I inquire about my children? Will they be transferred to this detention center, too?"

Mai's inner debate was brief. "I never had your children. I lied."

The eyes that came back to hers were angry and defiant, then something replaced that, something she thought might be gratitude. "*Allahu akbar*," he murmured. "Thank you for telling me."

"Just in case your new interrogators try that tactic, I know your children are safe in Pakistan in a place where the CIA or the U.S. military can't touch them. I've made sure of that."

He studied her, his eyes holding hers far longer than he ever had. "Why do you do this?" he asked again.

"I've already said you don't need to know that. Ask again, and I walk away." He didn't look away, but his jaw clenched. "Much better. Now, the one thing, the only thing that will get them to stop torturing you is to tell them *anything*."

Again, they stared at each other for several minutes, both still and silent, their breathing synchronized by chance, their faces without expression.

"Do you understand what I'm saying?" Mai asked him.

The emotion he, at last, showed in full was astonishment, but he nodded again. "I do not understand why—"

Mai held up a hand. "As much as I detest you, I detest injustice more." She stood, put the chair between them. "I won't wish you luck, and a part of me will rejoice when they kill you."

She turned to go, but his voice stopped her. "The first time you interrogated me, you said I had caused you grief. You, I never saw until you walked into this room that first time. How could I have caused you grief?"

The images of when she dug herself out of hell played nightly in her dreams and, when she wasn't careful, assaulted her when she was awake. A small concession was within interrogation protocols, and he should carry some burden of knowledge into the next stage of his life.

"I was in Number Two World Trade Center when it collapsed." That was all he needed to know, but she saw he didn't believe her. "There were times, here, in the middle of my nightmares, when I wanted to hold your severed head up for my camera, like you did the journalist's."

That he did believe. "Why did you not?" he asked.

"Because at some point, like now, I wanted you to know I had your life in my hands, but I showed you something you will never understand. Mercy."

The Sheik nodded again as he took in the words, then he lay a hand over his heart and said, "For your compassion, *Enshallah*, one day, I will see you in Paradise."

Mai laughed, and it unnerved the murderer before her. "No," she said, "More likely I'll see you in Hell."

After all, every night she was already there, and she was, if anything, patient. Some things were worth waiting for.

Enshallah.

St. Paul's Illumination

Jack Trammell

Jason was caught in the beam for the very first time when we were out deer hunting. I saw the light, a wavering reddish glow that seemed to rise steadily above the hardwoods at the top of Slate Ridge and then slowly glided toward us. I figured it was a helicopter, or one of those spy planes that are always coming over from Wright-Patterson. I remembered a story about Lt. Frank Patterson having been killed by a UFO in 1931 and that was why they named the base after him, so I figured UFOs and spy planes were one and the same.

But when the light was directly overhead, a blue beam came out and caught Jason full force. I heard him grunt, as if taking a hard hit playing football. His face contorted and he slumped over, like he had the stomach cramps, or was sick.

"Jason! Jason, are you OK?"

When I tried to move, it was as if my feet were joined to the ground. Even my thoughts inside my head seemed to be rooted together, stuck such that I couldn't separate them one from another, even though part of me could see each one for what it was. My vision started fading to black, and then there was nothing.

* * * *

"Blaine! Get over here! I found some more."

I moved over to where Jason was hunched over, and sure enough, there were more of the strangely twisted, spotted, brown lobster mushrooms beneath a wide granite ledge. We had hit the mother lode.

"How do you know for sure these are safe?" I asked.

"I know! These are good, good—look at the mottling. And we need to get them all. Don't miss any."

Since the "accident" Jason seemed to know a lot more about everything. I had never heard of lobster mushrooms, or morels, or chanterelles, or maitakes before. But now he knew

50

about all of them and could identify them instantly by sight. He even knew a few by their Latin names.

"How come you know so much about this?" I said. "I've never been here. You brought me right here."

"I read a book, Blaine. Don't look at me like I'm crazy. I *can* read."

* * * *

Perhaps it was all just coincidence, but Jason also switched jobs about this same time. He had been working at the Kroger store near Pitchtown, bagging groceries, but now he worked at the apothecary on Main Street. In fact, he told me that he was being trained to do Mr. Bloomington's job.

"You can't be a pharmacist!" I said. "You have to go to school to do that."

"Well, you can, in some cases," he insisted. "I know this on good authority. Mr. Bloomington himself told me that if I keep doing as well as I have, that he will have special permission granted until I can go to that school and get certification."

"Go to school? Jason, you never went to school even when technically you were enrolled! Go to school?"

"Blaine, you sound jealous or something—you aren't the only one who can go to college, you know."

He referred to my two years at Shepherd, degree uncompleted, which I someday hoped to continue.

"No," I said. "I suppose not."

* * * *

The other strange event involved breaking up with his long-time girlfriend, Lou Ann, whom everyone had assumed would become his wife once he worked full time. The poor girl was inconsolable, and yet Jason seemed completely indifferent, even cruel. Those of us who knew him could not reconcile all of the combined changes.

Jason, myself, and Richard Keel had met down at the abandoned mill to drink beer as we occasionally did, and the light showed up again, at first only producing a vague reddish haze that seemed to be just over the crest of the hill. It was just like before.

"Jason," Richard said, raising his can to sip, but his eyes locked on the light, "everyone says you've been acting strangely ever since that light's been coming around." He pointed up the hill. "I see it glowing right now, in fact. What did they do to you—take you away in a spaceship to do experiments with you?"

I watched Jason closely, and his black eyes seemed to flash. He crushed his own empty can and threw it into the stream, where it floated for a moment, and then disappeared beneath the dark surface.

"That's real funny, Dick. Very humorous. But I didn't go up into any alien spaceships. And I have no idea how that rumor got started."

Richard held his can out toward me. "Blaine said he was there the first time the light caught you."

"I didn't say that I saw him go up in a spaceship," I said quickly. "I only said that the light got him."

"The light got him?" Richard said. "What does that mean exactly? Something has to be making that light. Is it humans?"

"Come on," Jason said. "Both of you clowns come with me and I'll show you exactly what nonsense you're talking. Let's go up there and I'll show you."

Richard and I exchanged a glance. I know that I didn't want to go up there. Richard apparently didn't either.

"What's the matter?" Jason said. "You scared of little green men and flying saucers? Let's go. I'll show you how the light got me." He started treading the uneven path up the hill.

Richard and I waited, each for the other, to see who would go first. Finally, Richard leaned over and grabbed the last West Virginia ("That'll win ya!") from the edge of the water, popped the tab, and only peer pressure alone forced me follow him.

"Maybe he'll show us more mushrooms," I mumbled to myself.

* * * *

Later, we met at the diner near the apothecary over lunch to figure out what it all meant. Richard was angry; Jason indifferent; I was curious.

"So," I said, trying to be diplomatic, "you told us there weren't any little green men. You said you would show us what happened to you. All I remember is walking up the hill, feeling tired and slow, and then nothing."

"I remember that damned light!" Richard said. "When it came blue it changed. You said it wouldn't hurt anyone, but I feel sore all over, and it hurts when I go to the bathroom."

Jason smiled slightly. "You are fine, Dick, and you had that problem before last night, as a result of dating Melinda, I'm pretty sure."

"Shut up!" Richard said. But the curl on his lips belied his belief in that explanation, too.

"Back to the point," I said. "We don't know what happened to you, or to us. And if what I suspect is true, then all of us are in danger."

"Danger? What, pray tell, do you think happened?" Jason said, his eyes narrowing.

"There's something that happens when that light gets you—it makes you different than who you are—it changes you somehow. It's like you become someone else."

"That's utter nonsense," Jason said.

"How?" Richard said. "What do you mean, you become someone else, Blaine?"

Jason stood up abruptly, his food untouched. "Ladies, I must excuse myself. But I will say this: you are both overreacting to something that you should not be terrified about. This is the role that ignorance plays in the world. In fact, this is why it happens here in God's Country, and not in New York City, or Paris, France—because people here need enlightenment, and to naturally trust the knowledge that is given to them. I gave you my word no harm would come to you, and yet you still insist on your primitive stigma and fear. What would you have me do?"

When we didn't answer immediately, he stood up and left.

"Well, that went well," Richard said. "He's about as forthcoming as a guilty preacher."

"Come on," I said. "I want you to go to the doctor with me."

"Blaine, it's like an alien took him over or something!"

"Dick, we've got to get you checked out while you're still somewhat normal."

* * * *

It made any of us nervous to be at the doctor's office, but Dick particularly so. I could tell from the perspiration on his forehand and trembling hands that he was extremely uncomfortable, and I promised him free beer several times when he faltered on the way to the office.

"So," the doctor said, a bespectacled man we all knew well from our high school football physicals. "What brings you in, boys?"

Richard, like a sheep, crawled onto the examination table and sat in a slump.

"It's Richard, sir," I said. "He's been up on Slate Ridge with us and he caught the lights. I'm worried there's something wrong with him."

The doctor didn't blink, but instead began to poke and prod and use his stethoscope several different ways south of comfortable. Richard was still.

"Well," he said. "There's no harm in the lights. This place is famous for them. I'd be more worried about the crazies you might meet in the woods trying to take pictures of them." He motioned for Richard to stand up. "OK, drop 'em."

"Yes," the doctor continued, "the reporters are the worst. There's always something in their faces that says, 'We don't believe you hicks! If you can't even speak proper English with all the correct articles and niceties, then you certainly can't be a legitimate witness to the paranormal!' I submit to you that they are the paranormal here in this place."

Richard continued obediently while the examination continued. "I see you are recovering nicely from that bout with sailor's rash. . . . Do you need a refill?"

"Yes, sir."

"OK, back up on the table, please."

The doctor then ran his hand around Dick's skull and then peered deeply into each eye and ear using a magnifier viewer. Then he looked for what seemed like a long moment into Dick's face.

"Son, there is absolutely nothing wrong with you. What are you so worried about?"

Richard looked at me and I hastened to explain.

"He's worried that getting in the lights will make him like Jason."

The doctor stared at us, blinked, and then burst into laughter. Then he slapped his knee and followed up by slapping Dick on the knee.

"Don't worry," he said, still giggling, "one of you three had to get respectable first, and if it's the ghost lights that brought it on, then watch out!"

* * * *

The problem was that then the changes started in Richard. It began innocently enough with him starting to date Lou Ann exactly one week after he had been to see the doctor. Jason, oddly enough, seemed to approve, even though back in high school he had been terribly jealous of anyone approaching her.

Richard gradually become more distant, and he and Jason began going places without me, which they said meant nothing—we had always split up in different pairs—but they looked at me askance whenever I happened to show up. They frequently were busy with work, or had to do something because of their girlfriends, so fishing trips and beer drinking became rare events.

I felt like I was overreacting and being slightly paranoid, but one day when I happened to go into the drugstore and found Dick with Jason at the apothecary counter, the way they looked at me finally triggered some other kind of reaction.

"Hello, Blaine," Richard said. Jason nodded, pulling at his thin black tie.

"Hello," I said. "How are my best alien friends doing today? Got a lunch date scheduled on Uranus? A little beer drinking at the end of the galaxy?"

They looked at each other, trying to play the innocent.

"Blaine," Jason said, "we've been worried about you. You haven't been acting like yourself."

"You're darn right I haven't been acting like myself! I watched my two best friends get caught up in the lights, and now they're acting like zombies or something! It's infected your brains or something!"

Richard took a step toward me and placed his hand on my shoulder. "Blaine, I've been learning in my psychology class about blame shifting. This place—I know it's home, and we love it—but it's been stuck in a time warp. You've got to get out of that rut!"

"Quit blaming the lights," Jason said. "It's got nothing to do with it."

"It is the lights!" I insisted. "And, Dick, you agreed with me a few short weeks ago. You were terrified of them!"

"I'm not scared of those lights, Blaine. And you shouldn't be either."

Jason opened the waist-level door at the counter and came around to join us. He smiled.

"Come on, Blaine. Tonight, we'll get some beer, and all three of us go up to Slate Ridge, just like we always do, and we'll show you—those lights, if they're even there, are an anomaly."

"A what?"

"A natural occurrence without immediately apparent scientific explanation," Richard said. "But perfectly natural and harmless."

"This is what I mean!" I said. "You guys talk weird now!"

Jason sighed. "Growing up sucks, Blaine. But it happens anyway. We're still buddies, and we'll always have our trips. We'll meet you at the mill at the usual time." Jason smiled and patted me on the shoulder, just like Richard had done moments earlier.

I did not feel consoled. For a moment they looked identical to me; their faces, clothing, and smiles indistinguishable from each other. Then they were Richard and Jason again.

* * * *

The lights were out in full force. I arrived at the mill early, before dusk had settled into the sounds and smells of the night, and even then the reddish glow was faintly visible on the worn oak boards of the mill's walls. I tried not to look at it.

Dick and Jason appeared out of the darkness, at first only black shadows to me that seemed to move when you weren't looking directly at them. Then they ambled into the level before the broken dam and mill trace, both of them smiling. Each was carrying two six packs of West Virginia.

"Hey, planning a party, huh?" I said.

"Good times," Jason said. "Might as well enjoy them."

A strange memory came to me, from when we were much younger and Jason had called beer Dutch courage before we climbed across the river bridge on the girders. Apparently, they thought I would need courage.

"Guess those lights are here after all," Richard said. "But no worries, Blaine. I have another theory I'm working on. There's an abandoned mine up there on the east slope, and I think some kind of gas is leaking out from that and is interacting with the cooling air and magnetic properties of the rock to create that red effect."

"That so . . ." I said slowly.

Richard tossed me a can, while the rest was nestled in the rocks of the cool water. Soon the conversation was flowing freely and it was like old times. Jason, for some reason, had worn his work clothes up, and after his third beer, ceremoniously yanked his tie off and threw it into the mill waters. Richard did a caricature of his new boss. To my utter surprise, I watched the two of them trade nasty anecdotes about Lou Ann.

Then, when there was only one six pack remaining in the water, a silence came over all three of us, and you could clearly hear the sounds of the water bubbling through the rocks. I started to close my eyes, but a strong hand on each shoulder jolted me.

"OK, Blaine. Time to go see that the lights are harmless."

They literally lifted me onto my feet, and a surreal, stumbling journey up the trail began. The reddish lights wavered and fluoresced, as if dancing to the strange rhythms of music none of us could hear. I looked at everything along the way that meant not looking at the lights—the dark green laurel bushes like monsters in the half light, the boulders the size of cars, the craggy oaks that had dared to grow where nothing else would.

Then the blue beam erupted.

* * * *

The reporter seemed annoyed and disorganized. I waited patiently.

"Dr. Kirk—"

"Just call me Blaine, please."

"Blaine . . . I see here that you come originally from a very small town in Appalachia. Your fellow scientist and wife, Emma, is from France, right? And the two of you have been working on this particle acceleration project in collaboration with the United Nations for quite some time."

"Yes, that's right."

"I'm just curious, sir—when you were growing up back home, did you ever see yourself where you are today?"

I smiled.

Fishing

Sarah Collins Honenberger

Lila had never intended to live in the land of gaudy wall geckos and four o'clock early bird dinner deals. She'd never intended to be unemployed. Or divorced. Still, forty-nine years had yielded some small degree of practical experience, not necessarily wisdom. And it was quite clear to her it was easier to cut corners in a warm climate than a cold one. Goddamn Eric. She hoped her ex-husband was buried under ten feet of snow in that fancy leather chair in their Philadelphia townhouse. His townhouse, after the divorce settlement.

She dumped a second jigger of gin into the double-insulated glass. When the neon flamingos imbedded in the plastic netherworld smirked back at her, she stuck out her tongue. After she watched the tonic tumble energetically over the ice and drown the mangled lime, she took the drink out to the lanai, where the last of the sun lapped the edge of the yard. With too large a part of the settlement she'd bought the shingled cottage, painted it Tuscan colors on the inside and turquoise on the outside, and had sent the rest of the money to the financial adviser recommended by her college roommate. He happened to be Jennifer's brother and didn't remember Lila from college mixers. He spent a whole morning with her, flinging multicolored PowerPoint slides onto the big screen in his conference room, asking endless personal questions about her spending habits, her dreams, her health. Together they planned out her golden years.

And even though he propositioned her at lunchtime and she said no to that—he rooted for the Cowboys and was married to a sorority sister—Lila said yes to his advice about the mutual funds. Less risky, he'd said, and she felt better immediately. It didn't last.

When the first online statement showed up in her e-mail, she saved it to a folder labeled "K Ching" to foil identity fraud criminals. Until Eric's affair and the divorce, she had never worried, about finances or otherwise. They both had careers, no children, no gambling habits. But here in a strange town in a new house, even with the security system installed in the cottage for $49.95 a month, she worried all the time. One sleepless night she calculated how long she could live on the investment account. She was shocked to learn that at the rate she was going, with no job and the taxes and utilities at the house—AC in Florida way more expensive than she'd anticipated—the money would run out before her fifty-sixth birthday.

That same night she posted the Craigslist ad for a roommate. Nooney, short for Edward Morris Noonan, was the third person to respond, and he came right over. A broad-shouldered Irishman, whose divorce had been more expensive than hers because he'd fought back. He was working two jobs and seeking comfort in all the wrong places. She didn't ask about his overnights away because she felt lucky to have not stumbled on a serial killer. Nooney was kind and sympathetic and he didn't make fun of her phobia about a break-in. He remembered to double lock the door when he came in, even from washing his car, and whenever he was home he insisted on looming in the open doorframe while she walked Jeepers after the evening news.

"Lila? You here?" It was Nooney home from his day job, checking on her before he showered, changed, and sped away to the night shift at the Gucci grocery store, where he restocked shelves for $12 an hour. "Hey," he called from the kitchen door. "Drinking again?"

"Hey yourself." She raised her glass in a mock toast. "How was the office?"

It was an inside joke. She knew very well he sold AFLAC out of his car. It seemed like a dead end to her. He said it paid for his Bluetooth and his wireless. She wasn't sure it paid for much else. After he rubbed the dog's belly with the bottom of his shoe, he took off his seersucker sport jacket, careful to tweak the shoulders so it lay unwrinkled on the back of the lawn chair. He stretched out on the glider. The impracticality of a light-colored jacket if dry cleaning was not in your budget struck her anew. He wasn't terribly good at decisions. But then again, she had walked away from a two-million-dollar house because she couldn't face breakfast with a man who'd been having cyber sex with a woman in Hawaii for two years while his wife of twenty-four years nursed his elderly father through Alzheimer's.

"Big plans?" Nooney asked.

"Hardly. My back's killing me. I didn't want to spend the thirty dollars for the chiropractor so I opted for a hot shower and a Red Box. The G and T is dinner."

"Romantic comedy or shoot 'em up?"

"There is nothing funny about romance."

"My sentiments exactly. Where were you when I was standing at the altar?"

She took a gulp of the cold drink and let the fizz wiggle down into her chest. The concrete was warm under her bare feet. Jeepers stretched out in the sun. Florida wasn't all bad.

"Nooney? Can I ask you a personal question?"

"They're all personal at my age."

"How old are you exactly?"

"Sixty-one, but I'm often mistaken for a twenty-nine-year-old."

She thought "often" was an exaggeration, not his first. He had an amazing capacity for being optimistic, considering his situation. Still he was alive, employed, and eating regularly. She, on the other hand, would be homeless in six years.

"Why twenty-nine?"

"Thirty sounds ancient to the coeds, and twenty-nine sounds established."

She sighed. Why did even halfway smart men think with the wrong part of their anatomy?

She jiggled the glass so the ice would spin and collapse and she could manage another mouthful of liquid before she had to decide whether she would sink to a second one. "How do you stay so upbeat and happy?"

"That's question number two." He pointed to her glass as he pushed himself up and out of the rusted glider. "Can I fix you another?"

"Is that your answer?"

"No," he laughed in that cheery, brittle way he had of tossing off the pain she caught in his eyes when he thought she wasn't looking. "You are a ridiculous woman. Happiness is a thing that happens to you. You can't stitch it up out of whole cloth and wishful thinking."

"That sounds like love."

"Happiness is a better bet, I think. Being the unlovable person I am, if my ex-wife is correct."

She felt terrible for having brought it up. His wife had drained all the confidence out of him and taken all his money. Yet he woke up every day and hung the Bluetooth over his ear, went out into the world, and repeated the insurance mantra a hundred times for very few sales. Dying at fifty-six didn't seem quite so awful, now that she thought about it. Or was that the G and T talking?

In the morning Nooney was gone when she woke up, the Bluetooth crooner silent. She padded around the house in her bare feet, wishing she had a job to rush off to. Her waking vow to be more positive was already fading into obscurity with the reality of being alone in a house she couldn't afford. She marveled at the wall of palm leaves that screened the sun outside her windows and left startling patterns on her blank walls and floors. She had left the furniture behind in Philadelphia—too many memories. Even the empty cottage, which had charmed her at first with its potential, reminded her of Eric and failure merely because it was something they hadn't shared, emphasizing his absence.

While she stood by the window, she reminded herself of the vow. She circled four employment notices in the want ads before she let herself be distracted by the ripples on the fishpond, a cobalt blue vinyl pool buried in the sand and surrounded by yucca in assorted sizes to lend it a more natural look. The koi had come with the house, perhaps the residue of someone else's divorce.

The constant circling of the big fish terrified her, like sharks targeting their prey. In the last seven months since she'd arrived they'd doubled in size. And while it was impossible to count exactly, it seemed as if one or maybe two were missing. With each Creamsicle flash in the water, she was reminded they were watching her too. Even as she clicked away at the keyboard, licking the edge of her coffee mug for the last dregs of hazelnut creamer, listing her work experience, tabbing ever so professionally through the job applications from the paper, she could feel the damp ponderous eye of the koi following her every move.

As soon as she finished at the computer she would get rid of them. It was a brainstorm. With a rush of high school keyboarding prowess she ran through the details of her last two jobs, the more permanent prior home address in Philadelphia, and her references, all from Pennsylvania. Was that the reason she'd had no interview calls? Equatorial mind-set couldn't raise the energy to contact someone somewhere as foreign and distant as a state above the Mason-Dixon line?

At least she had work experience. At least she was being honest. She hadn't been fired or downsized. She'd chosen to relocate, that was all, hardly a reason to overlook a perfectly qualified candidate who just happened to be middle aged. Anyway, there was a law against that. She did wonder if her ambivalence about the job descriptions came across in her applications. She took a deep breath. Wondering wasn't getting her hired. She needed to bottle Nooney's optimism and try harder.

After she changed into shorts and a T, she ravaged the garage for the fishing net she knew she'd seen when she stored the boxes of Christmas decorations and college books and winter sweaters, things that belonged to her former life.

"Ah-hah," she yelled when she found the net, on a pole as long as a broom handle, hidden in the rafters. The former tenant had been good at using every available space. On her tiptoes she stood on the boxes and wiggled the net loose. With the shovel, an old spackle bucket, and the fishing net in hand, she trekked back to the fishpond.

"Prepare to be relocated," she announced. She wasn't going to hurt them, despite the Hemingway daydreams. The net, of course, was too small. The yucca blades stabbed her from every side. Kneeling was impossible. She yanked out a pile of water lilies for a clearer view, but she wasn't having any luck. If koi ran out of space, they might eat each other, but they didn't eat humans. Still the idea of stepping into the murky water made her stomach flip. There had to be another way.

An hour into it—she guessed this from the overhead spotlight of noonday sun—the phone rang in her pocket. A friendly vibrating tingle on her thigh. Maybe a prospective employer, though it seemed unlikely given the dozens of unanswered applications she'd submitted over the last seven months and the proximity of this morning's Internet filings. Maybe it was her mother calling, dangerously close to dementia but still with enough of her faculties to use the cell phone to complain about her crazy neighbors in the nursing home.

Lila ignored the phone. The koi project was this morning's challenge. She always could prioritize, no matter what Eric said about her drifting along in her career, not being aggressive enough to seek out promotions. She, at least, was in full command of her faculties and only forty-nine, perfectly able to rid herself of the enemy at the gate. She might not be able to muscle the koi, but she could trick them. They were fish after all.

Nooney whistled when he didn't see her in her usual chair on the lanai. Deep in thought about the next step, she didn't reply. The three koi were in separate black plastic trash bags, the thick kind advertised to hold up to fifty pounds of construction debris. She'd found the bags also in the magical garage. The pool was drained, its slick green slime baking in the afternoon sun. Blood streaks ran down her legs like Cirque du Soleil tights. She was crying as she Googled on her phone to find a place to deliver the koi. Animal shelters in three counties had said no, they didn't accept fish. She wasn't sure how long the koi would last with the amount of water she'd managed to sluice into the bags after she'd shoveled their foot-long bodies along the slippery pool bottom and into the open mouths of the bags, stretched wide with fish line tied around the legs of the wrought iron chairs. She had been careful not to hurt them. She certainly didn't want them to die.

She hated being alone. She hated Florida and the goddamn constant cheerful sun. She hated the whiny helpless person she had become.

"Wow," Nooney said, the same seersucker sport coat draped over his shoulder. He looked like a J.Crew ad, except for a new nickel-sized coffee stain blatant on one cuff. The poor guy. "Cleaning the fishpond means you're either feeling desperate or invincible. Did you get a job?"

"I have no idea. I've been out here all day, fighting these stupid fish. The phone's rung four times and I couldn't answer it because . . . because . . ." She held up her filthy hands.

One of the black bags shot into the air ten inches and dropped back hard on the pool bottom.

"You put the koi in there?" Nooney asked. "That's impressive."

"I've never liked them. But I can't find anyone who wants them and they're heavier than I expected. I've wasted the whole day. I guess I'll have to refill the pond and let them out."

He flexed his right arm like a wrestler. "I have fifteen minutes. But if we put them in the trunk of your car, they won't last long. You better figure out quickly where you're going."

Right there on the patio, he stripped down to his boxers. He hung each piece of clothing on the chair with great deliberation. He folded the slacks on the crease, tweaked the shoulders of the shirt and the jacket in turn, and slipped the dress shoes side by side under the chair, one sock in each shoe.

"You don't look a day over twenty-nine," she said.

"And you look like you're twelve, up to your elbows in mud." His grin was infectious. "Before I join you in that mess, I think we need a tarp, something we could put the fish, ah . . . pet carriers on and then drag over to the car. Do we have one?"

She scrambled through mental images of the garage. "I think there's one covering the bicycles."

When he returned he had an old horse blanket, striped earth tones and thick, and a bright blue plastic tarp, bundled around his arms like a little girl's furry muff.

"You are a magician," she said.

"That would be more useful than an insurance salesman with a bad heart."

"You have a bad heart? Why didn't you say something? Oh, Nooney, I'm so sorry."

"Just don't tell the coeds." He sat on the vinyl edge and let his pale, bony legs swing down. "Yuck," he said when his toes reached the mud. "All day, seriously?"

She saw how silly it looked. Eric would say she had lost her mind. He paid people to do things because he didn't like to get his hands dirty. He'd never understood that April feeling of wonder when the daffodils opened and she just had to be out digging in the garden. Even Nooney was looking at her like she was kooky.

He plowed ahead, though. He laid the plastic tarp on the bottom of the pool. After he tucked the edges under the first trash bag, he slid the shovel under the bag from the opposite end until it hit the weight of the fish. His feet made slurpy sounds in the muck. "If you pull the top of the bag up at this same end where I'm standing, I think it, he, it will slide the other way."

She saw that, if it worked, the fish and the bag would be on the tarp. "I should have figured that out." She grabbed a handful of plastic and tugged gently.

"Two heads," he muttered, with soft jabs of the shovel under the bag as if he were prodding a child to jump off the diving board. For several seconds nothing changed and then, with a lovely satisfyingly loud swish the water, the fish gurgled away from their feet and smacked noisily into the opposite wall of trash bag. "Ta Da." He put his leg against the bag to keep the fish from sliding backward.

"Now all we have to do," she announced in her cheeriest voice, "is keep the bag on the tarp while we pull them both up over the lip of the pool. Then drag it to the car, lift it into the trunk, and do the whole thing two more times, drive like a banshee to a pond or a lake, and dump them without being arrested for trespassing, all before the greedy things die of exposure."

He laughed.

She could see how funny it was. "You better go and shower. I don't want you to be late on account of your crazy landlady's scheme to rid herself of a few bothersome cannibals. I think I can manage from here."

"I'm really sorry I have to abandon you," he said.

"No you're not." She laughed with him.

While he was showering and after she washed her hands with the hose, she moved the car as close to the pond as it could be with the palm trees and the garden rocks. She left the trunk open. With a rope she found in the garage, she threaded the sprockets on the tarp, cinched it up, and tied a knot. It looked like a huge blue pot sticker.

"Disgusting." She'd been talking to herself for hours now, a sure sign of dementia. Which reminded her of her mother, which reminded her of this morning's unanswered phone calls.

Standing in the shade, she fished the phone out of her pocket and covered her eyes from the glare while she dialed voicemail. One message from her mother. The nurse had poisoned her and her toes were turning cerulean. She hadn't ever heard her mother use the word cerulean. Old people could too learn new skills. Three messages from Ms. Lisinger at the county school board office. They liked her resume, didn't need a guidance counselor per se, but could use someone to help with the seniors' college applications. They thought she'd be a good fit.

Lila whooped it up a little, spinning around the patio table, and doing a very bad version of an Indian rain dance. She was still dancing when Nooney came out in khakis and a golf shirt, his regular uniform for the grocery job. His hair was wet, combed neatly, and his cheeks were ruddy.

"You are fast," she said, when she'd actually been thinking how handsome he was, but knew better than to go there.

"I should have called in sick and stuck with you."

"No, this is my project. I'll do it."

"What happened? You were ready to give up fifteen minutes ago."

"An interview. I have an interview. Tomorrow, first thing. It's the high school. They need someone in guidance to help with college applications. Part-time for now, but if it works into more, there's the possibility of state retirement."

"You're already thinking about retirement and you haven't even started working?"

"I'm not really thinking about retiring, just thinking about the future. This could be a new beginning."

"Then we should celebrate. I'm off tomorrow. If you're not in jail for abandoning the koi in some protected public wetlands, I'll take you to dinner. Dutch treat if that's OK with you. It'll have to be somewhere not too fancy."

"Not one of those early bird specials?"

"Hell, no, I'm only twenty-nine, remember? And you're way too young to be a senior."

"I might not get the job."

"Well, there's always Animal Warden. You caught them, you released them to the wild."

"Oh, my God, the koi. They're probably roasting in those bags."

Nooney didn't wait, but, now that they'd worked out the system, she was positive she could finish it on her own.

Playing Nightly

Elaine Ruggieri

Ray Ballantine stands outside the cocktail lounge, staring at his glossy print on the billboard. It's a slick, stylish presentation, bald spots airbrushed away, wrinkles and eye sags smoothed, the sequined lapels of his tuxedo sparkling. Seated at his glitter-dusted piano, his head is tilted and his eyebrows are slightly arched in surprise. "Think of someone you cherish," the clever photographer had suggested. He thought of Vicky.

A print of this same photo sits in a desk drawer in his office, in a manila envelope stamped Do Not Bend. But he will never send it to Vicky. Her husband might see it. On the bottom, right-hand corner, with a Sharpie pen, he wrote, "Victoria Regina, always in my mind. Ray Ballantine." He used indigo blue ink to contrast with the glossy black and white, evoking midnight and romance, he thought. His signature swirled with loopy flourishes to draw her attention to his name.

Ray turns with a sigh and walks to the elevators to read the hotel's events directory. If there's a convention or banquet tonight, it will be a lively evening in the lounge. That kind of crowd gets rowdy with booze and sometimes sings and dances to his music. He prepares for each night in the lounge by thinking of the music the hotel guests might like to hear.

An entry in the middle of the list catches his eye, and he reads, "Shenandoah Valley Apple Growers Association Banquet—Main Ballroom." Could Vicky's brother, who owns an orchard, be here, Ray wonders, swallowing now with difficulty. He leans against the wall to steady himself. He ran into her brother Dom before at this hotel and introduced himself as an old friend from The Players. The brother said something about a long time ago and performing only once with the summer stock group, but he did seem to recall Ray at the piano during rehearsals. He cheerfully informed Ray, after being prompted about Vicky, that his sister was living in Fairfax. Her husband had a terrific job, and they had two wonderful kids.

But, how is Vicky wearing her hair? Ray wanted to ask. Is the thick ponytail still swinging rhythmically as she walks or dances or even laughs heartily at one of his jokes? Does she still have that confident, fast stride? Still using the same shampoo that he now uses for a pungent reminder? The brother said he'd tell Vicky that Ray said hello, shook his hand, and walked away.

At the entrance of the ballroom, Ray listens to spoons and forks bumping plates, waiters banging trays, and diners raising a steady roar of laughter and conversation. He is watching a man at the head table with black, thick hair like Vicky's. He wants to move closer to see if the man has the same dark brows and bright eyes like hers, the same high forehead that recedes when greeting people, the eyes that widen when smiling. The last time he talked to her brother here, Ray stood watching him and waiting, thinking any second Vicky would step out of her brother's body and then laugh at her marvelous trick.

Ray walks to the upright piano near the head table and pretends to select music from the books in the bench. He can see the man closely now. His hair is dark but curly, and he is much too young. It must be ten years ago when I last talked to Dom, Ray thinks. Ten years! Everyone changes. Has Vicky? Ray selects some sheet music and leaves the ballroom.

Before entering the cocktail lounge, he brushes lint off his shoulders, tugs at his shiny lapels, and smiles quickly at his reflection in the dark window of the swinging door.

"Like what you see?" asks a waitress passing through. She doesn't wait for an answer, and the familiar beery, stale air swings with her toward him. He keeps walking to the bar.

"Hey, Ray! Not many now, but it'll be packed when that banquet lets out. Big sales meeting upstairs too. Remember, those guys closed up the joint last night. And, loud! Phew!" the bartender Pete says and sets a cup of black coffee in front of him.

"Yeah, so what else is new?" Ray asks and takes a sip.

"Uh oh. Maybe you better drink something stronger. Bad day? I was only trying to—"

Ray shakes his head. "Don't mind me, Pete. Just thought I saw someone I knew. Memories, you know?" He hopes Pete will continue cutting lemon slices or go to the other end of the bar to gossip with the waitstaff. He doesn't want to talk. Pete always does. His cell phone vibrates. It's a text from his wife. "Will be late. Can't call tonight. Playing bridge. Weather sunny." He doesn't reply, just shrugs.

"Yeah, memories," says Pete. "Some good, some bad. How long you been playin', Ray? Ever get tired of all those young women moonin' over ya? What's the wife think? You work all day; you're here every night. Some life!" Pete wipes the bar as he speaks.

"No worse than yours," says Ray, staring at his coffee.

"Don't I know it?" Pete finishes the lemons and now slices oranges. He looks up at Ray. "You must be pushing sixty. You really like pounding those keys that much? Or, maybe it's just those women moonin' over ya." He laughs. "Gotta be better than sloshing whiskey and listening to drunks."

"Maybe. Been at it since high school," says Ray, wincing at the hot coffee. "Saturday night dances. Weddings. Amateur productions. Orchestras. Proms. Whatever. The wife got tired of it long ago."

"She oughta come here. We could use a good-looking woman around this place. Hell, I'd even buy her a drink."

"She'd rather be in Florida. No interest in my gig here." Ray shrugs. He shrugs a lot these days. It ends awkward conversations.

Pete shakes his head. "Wives!" he says.

Ray looks at his watch. Business is slow in the lounge at this hour, but he enjoys the eight o'clock set. The customers aren't quite ready to listen, and he can warm up. He glances around the room. Some of the sales men and women, with their "hello" tags dangling, are standing at the bar, drinking highballs and swapping tales of colossal deals. Tables of women in business attire nurse exotic concoctions as Pete's citric samples hang from their glasses. An elderly man, with a much younger, blonde woman, works on his supersized martini. The usual hooker is doing early reconnaissance. At this hour, Ray will play robotically as the customers down their cocktails before dinner, if they ever order dinner. He will rehearse for the second show and think, dream, of Vicky, as he plays.

He remembers her standing off stage. It was dark. The other dancers and singers were crowded about them. He was right behind her. "Hi," he said, leaning toward her right ear, smelling her freshly shampooed hair.

"Oh, Ray. Hi. I'm so nervous. This number always goes wrong," she said, looking up at him. Someone shushed them and he was shoved into her. He gently grabbed her small waist. "I'm sorry. Someone keeps pushing me."

She giggled, and a dancer next to her said, "God, I'm so hungry! I need a burger and a shake."

"Me, too," said Vicky. "And fries!" She gave her head a toss, and her ponytail lightly brushed his face as the scent of her clean hair wafted by. He wanted to embrace her, but stopped. She was a young twenty-one. He was thirty-three and married, an accountant by day, piano player by night. Smitten since the first day of tryouts for an amateur production, he wanted to be next to her every minute, adoring her youth, longing for her, showing off his piano talent during rehearsals. His infatuation amazed him, disgusted him, but amused him too. He idolized her. Whispering again beside her ear, he said, "Victoria, Victoria Regina. Queen of the Chorus."

She turned toward him with a wide smile. "Some queen all right. I'm scared stiff." He squeezed her waist and she ran, entering the stage on cue.

Pete is drying glasses and looking for water spots. "Guess you're ready to give them keys some hell. Sure you don't want a little kick. Scotch?" Ray goes back to his coffee.

"So, the wife got tired of it, huh? Can't please women, no how. If you don't work, you're lazy. Work too much, and they say they never see ya. My old lady tells me to get a day job. I tell her she's lucky I'm workin' day or night. When I'm home, she's mad and not talking, or talking so much, my ears hurt." Ray is quiet. "Oh, come on, Ray. Have a drink on the house."

Ray shakes his head and pushes his cup toward Pete. "Later, Pete. Time to start. Want to turn on the spot?"

There is no applause as he sits down at the piano. "Oh, look! We're going to have some music," one of the suited women says, following with a fake laugh. Ray smiles at her. He tests the mike, checks his glistening cuffs, and stretches his fingers.

"Good evening, ladies and gentlemen. I am Ray Ballantine, playing nightly here at the James River Lounge. I play old favorites and new hits. Oldies, goldies, anything you want to hear. Just tell the waitstaff." One of the younger waiters points to himself and waves to the crowd, mouthing "Me!" The young blonde with the older man waves back. Ray leans toward the mike and says, "Hope you enjoy it."

His fingers glide rapidly through a medley of old and new melodies and then press the keys to "Somewhere My Love." The billboard photo comes to life. His head moves in rhythm and his tux glimmers in the spotlight. Somewhere Victoria, he thinks. Doing what? Somewhere in Fairfax? Maybe. God, that summer was so long ago! She got married, had kids, and I'm still crunching numbers and pounding keys, pining for her like a schoolboy. "Earth Angel, will you be mine?" I should play that tonight. The seniors will love it.

Ray continues playing easy-listening numbers. "Lawrence Welk without the corn," his wife once described his act. He can feel that the crowd is inattentive, more interested in their drinks; it's still too early. He blinks at the spotlight and smiles at the rear wall, where he imagines Vicky, standing and smiling back at him. The same suited woman says to her friends, "He can really play, can't he? And, good-looking too, for his age." He doesn't hear her friends respond.

Ray called Vicky once, a few years ago. When she answered, he started singing, "It was just one of those things, just one of those crazy—"

She recognized his voice right away and said his full name, "Ray Ballantine! I can't believe it." He sighed and his hand got moist on the phone.

"Oh, yes, Victoria Regina, Queen of the Chorus, it is I. That song reminds me of you. Is your hair still glossy black? Lustrous satin? Mood indigo?" He didn't recognize his own voice. He was lightheaded. She gave the usual little laugh before she answered, pretending his compliments were exaggerated, never serious.

"No gray hairs yet, but these kids might turn it white any day now," she said, again deflecting any hint of knowing Ray's emotions, but he felt she was always aware. He wondered if he frightened her.

"How's that dancer's figure?" Ray quickly asked. He didn't want to hear about her kids.

"Well, my old clothes still fit, but—"

"Vicky, I think of you every night I play." He heard a child crying, not too far away.

"Gotta go, Ray. Sorry. It's been wonderful talking to you. Glad you're OK. Thanks for calling."

"Good-bye, dear," he said, not OK, but relieved he no longer heard her child wanting her.

Ending the set with the fast-tempo theme from *The Sting*, Ray gives the keys an abrupt push on the last chord. After acknowledging the little applause, he quickly leaves the spotlight and heads to the bar. "Hi, Doll," says the same teasing waitress. "Play one just for me next set. You know, 'A Fool in Love'?" He nods to her and moves on. Pete is waiting for him with a fresh cup of coffee.

"These people tonight are dry as camels. Banquet's over and now they're really thirsty." He fills the ice bin. "Some man was here looking for you, Ray. Said he'd be back. No name." Can't be Dom, Ray thinks. Some musician, probably playing a private party somewhere else in the hotel. If only Vicky were looking for him! He would play all her favorites. Their favorites, he liked to think.

He remembers a time he did play just for her. The Red Bud Inn in Nellysford. He had just finished a set, and a waitress dropped a napkin on his piano. The spotlight was still on so he could hardly see the writing. "Just one of those crazy things finding you here tonight. V." While studying the small wavy scrawl, he heard her voice behind him. "Ray Ballantine! Remember me?" God, if she only knew! And, there she was— dark hair, bright eyes, wide smile, but no ponytail. She took his trembling hand and led him to a table to meet her husband. Her husband—Ray could never remember his name or didn't want to—said he'd heard a lot about Ray and his music. He shook his

74

hand, said it was good to meet him, and then left for the men's room.

"Vicky, I can't believe it. A dream come true!"

"I saw in Dom's paper that you were playing here, and I told my husband, we had to go, and . . ."

Ray kept staring. "That smile and those twinkling eyes! Oh, Vicky! I can never forget Victoria Regina, Queen of . . ." He didn't finish. He saw her eyes narrow as she looked down. He knew he had said too much, and his disrespect shamed them both. He quickly resumed his guarded role of Prince Charming to his queen, adoring uncle to favorite niece, indulgent doter to endearing ingénue. Looking at her, a mature, married woman, he realized their age difference, unspoken and undeniable, had become irrelevant, but her marriage and his were not.

His coffee is getting cold, and he ignores it. "Hi, Ray. How ya doin'?" He turns and sees a former neighbor. Their wives had been good friends.

"Bob, what are you doing here? How's Grace? The kids?" Ray asks, realizing now Bob's the one who asked for him earlier, not Vicky's brother, Dom, as he had hoped.

"Everyone's great. I'm here for the apple growers meeting. Don't grow 'em, just sell 'em. How's your wife?"

"The same. Lots of bridge and vacations in Florida. Never comes here." Ray shrugs.

"Bars aren't my thing either. Just thought I'd say hi. Take care," he says and shakes Ray's hand.

"Thanks for coming by. Good to see you." Ray tries the stale coffee and makes a face at Pete, pointing to the cup.

"Well, I offered you a drink," says Pete. Ray shakes his head, leaves the bar, and walks through the tables to the piano for his last set.

He hears the suited woman say as he passes by, "Oh, listen up, girlfriends, here he comes again." Ray nods toward their table, making no eye contact with her. He knows how to avoid the type but still appear friendly. Sitting on the middle keys is a business card with a message. "Room 371" and signed, "The woman in the blue suit." He moves the card off the keys and addresses the crowd.

"Good evening, ladies and gentlemen. I'm Ray Ballantine, playing nightly here at the James River Lounge. I play whatever you want to hear. Old favorites and new hits. Oldies, goldies, you name it. Just give your requests to the waitstaff."

Straightening his satin bow tie, then stretching his fingers, he begins the intro and, with a change of pace, segues into "YMCA." It usually gets them on their feet. The women in suits leave their table and rush to stand in the spotlight. They're laughing and making awkward YMCA letters. A few salesmen join them. At the end of the number, they get their drinks and toast Ray. He gives a little bow and continues his repertoire. The flirty waitress approaches, winks, and hands him a napkin.

"A request! Let's see if I can read it," he says, holding the napkin out of the spotlight's glare. "Oh. 'Just one of those things.' Signed 'V'." He drops the napkin and looks anxiously at the crowd. Is she here? He feels the heat of the spotlight on his face and his breath quickens.

"Thank you, Vic. I mean Miss, Ms., or Mr. V. It's one of my favorites too." The audience has perked up, lots of loud laughing and talking. Ray always plays as if Vicky were near and the familiar love songs written just for them. Now he does short arrangements of "You Made Me Love You" and "The Way We Were." As he imagines her listening, sitting at one of the tables, he winks and flirts at the spotlight. It's too blinding for him to make out faces. He's perspiring. Where is she?

His fingers move effortlessly now. His timing is perfect and the audience quiets down, paying attention to his inspired music. He finishes the set with V's requested song, giving it his best treatment, once with his fingers pounding out a syncopated rhythm, then adding romantic arpeggios, and ending by accentuating the melody and singing the lyrics softly. The crowd applauds enthusiastically. Bowing, he dabs the perspiration off his face with V's napkin and puts it in his pocket. His throat is dry, but instead of going straight to the bar, he walks between tables, searching for Vicky. She's got to be here!

He hears his name and turns quickly. The older man, holding another double martini while hugging the younger blonde, is calling him. "Ray Ballantine. Ray." He puts his glass down. "Come on over here. I just want to thank you for playing

76

that last song. Valerie, my fiancée, requested it. Didn't you, honey?" He rests his balding head against hers and she kisses his forehead.

Ray estimates V for Valerie to be fiftyish, the man around sixty-five. "I just love that song. And you played it just right. Brings back memories," says Valerie, pushing back her big hair of yellow curls and wetting her lips with her tongue.

"Sure does," says Ray. "Glad you enjoyed it. Come back soon!" He turns quickly and bumps into the teasing waitress, who whispers, "Room 371. Wow-ee!" and moves on with a big grin.

Ray hurries to the bar in time to stop Pete from pouring him another coffee. He wants a double scotch, tall glass—harder to spill with shaking hands and racing heart. Pete sets him up and Ray takes a long drink. "Good scotch. Thanks, Pete. Needed that."

"I could tell. You look a little peaked, as my mother used to say. Guess the rush is over," says Pete. "Thirsty people, my God! I think every other order was a cosmo. How those women drink those sweet things beats me! I'll take beer any time, and it's time for one right now."

Pete opens a bottle, takes a swig, and leans across the bar toward Ray. "I heard about Room 371. How come you're so lucky?" He winks.

"Me? Lucky? You know that kind of woman. They just like to get attention," says Ray, "and see if I'll fall for it. Nothing new." He takes out his phone. No messages.

"When's the wife get back from Florida? Guess it's nice down there. My old lady says we should retire there. Retirement? That's for rich people. And, Florida! So, they got oranges."

"The wife plays cards there," says Ray with a shrug. "I play here." He finishes his scotch and waves to Pete as he leaves the bar. "See you tomorrow night."

Second Encounter

Lauvonda Lynn M. Young

The thought of reuniting with my high school classmates after thirty years has me in a tizzy. I keep reminding myself it is only a class reunion, but this gathering is different in that it's our first reunion since graduation. We probably are the only class in the history of our school that hasn't scheduled reunions with regularity. Everyone likely will be shocked to see how middle age has homesteaded in our bodies. While I don't mind aging, I hope we can conjure up more interesting topics of conversation tonight, because spending hours with a room full of overripe classmates, talking about wrinkles and constipation, will force me to guzzle the two bottles of Pinot Grigio stored under the front seat of my car without sharing a drop with anyone.

l arrived yesterday and elected to lodge at the Bluefield, West Virginia, Holiday Inn, instead of at the Comfort Inn located in Bluefield, Virginia, where the reunion is being held and where I figure most of my classmates will be staying. For some reason, I wanted to avoid running into anybody I know. It's not that I have a reason to dodge anyone. Maybe I just need more time to calm my nerves. I don't understand why I'm so anxious about a dang class reunion. Probably the only time my nerves would be more feverish would be if Elvis was giving me a big squeeze.

After searching out a parking space in the crowded parking lot at the Comfort Inn, I take a quick look in the mirror to confirm that every hair is in place. Lipstick is reapplied. My makeup is prefect already, but I dab some more powder on my face and chin. l sniff my armpits to see if there are sweat odors. There aren't any, but as a preventive measure I add extra squirts of perfume. It's time to exit my worn Mustang—time to abandon my comfort zone.

The hideous decorations assault my eyes as I enter the cramped event room. I think I've stepped back into time. From all appearances, it is the same embellishments we had at our senior prom—probably the stuff has been hibernating in one of our classmate's moldy basement waiting to serve a useful purpose. There are green and white streamers, our class colors, hanging from the ceiling, most of them moving gently because of the air generated from fans. A banner with the words "Welcome, Tazewell High School Classmates" is taped across the back wall. Tables loaded with food and beverages hug the same wall. Square tables, set up in rows, are covered with a white plastic cloth. All have been dotted with a large lighted candle and a small vase full of fake flowers. These items all look used, too, and I'm wondering if they have been living in the same basement. I don't know why the planning committee wasn't a little more creative. I would have thrown a little money in the pot for new decorations. Maybe the theme is supposed to remind us of the 1960s. Forget that. Hells bells, I hope we've all matured beyond those years. Maybe I shouldn't be too critical about the decorations, though. After all, I was too busy to volunteer to help with the planning and preparations. The truth is I could have helped, but I didn't want to get involved. Anyway, it won't kill me to reminisce for one evening. It might be fun to revisit a time when life was more carefree, but I sure can contribute if anyone wants to talk about tragedy, as I've survived my fair share. The worst trauma I've experienced was the unexpected death of my spouse, Rodney, four years ago. While I have plenty of pain to talk about, I really don't want to talk about death and other unpleasant things tonight. I've done my grieving.

Bobby Docks, who used to play 45 and 78 records at our school events, is our DJ. Of course, the words "disc jockey" didn't exist all those years ago, at least in the small town where I was born and lived until I was eighteen. Docks stuffed his equipment in the left corner of the room, next to the food tables. He always was the first one in line to get to the food. His pudginess has ballooned into obesity, but fatness is far more acceptable when a man wears it. I wonder if Docks ever married. He always had a flock of female friends, but this was probably because he was one of the few guys who had a vehicle and gas money, and he always was willing to truck us around. His equipment has been upgraded. Now he has a big box with huge speakers on each side. He has added a microphone for announcing songs. I wave, but Docks is busy fiddling with his equipment. "Love me Tender" fills the air. Docks always has known how much I adore Elvis. Since he used to have a crush on me, I'm betting he will play Elvis tunes all night. The thought brings a smile to my face.

A man and woman I don't recognize want me to move. I ask to be pardoned before I step aside to begin searching the room for familiar faces and a place to settle my butt. My anxiety level gets upped a few notches when I see my old boyfriend, James Stonewall Jackson. I am surprised to see him because he was in college when we dated. I suppose Freda Smyth invited him. They are dancing, pressed together like two pancakes, glued with syrup. Freda is molded to Stonewall the same way she attached herself to guys back in high school, when she wore all those tight sweaters that caused immense swooning.

Freda was our class tart. Her hair used to be a mousy brown, long and straight. It often looked in need of a shampoo. She matured into a frizzed, brassy blonde, with permed and overteased hair cut in a style long rejected by any female wanting to appear younger than her actual years. Freda's body still is terrific. She is wearing a skin-hugging strapless red dress; her ample breasts appear intent on escaping out the top of it. She pretty much continues to perpetrate the look of a loose woman. My guess is Freda has some stories to tell; life probably hasn't been too good to her.

Stonewall is engrossed in conversation with Freda. Their faces are close enough to kiss. I'm sure Stonewall wouldn't mind undergoing a few tongue exercises with Freda. He has aged, but he hasn't lost his looks. His white hair is neatly groomed and free of bald spots. Stonewall appears shorter than I remember him, which I suppose can be attributed to weight gain. At least he doesn't have a fat beer gut. All in all, he remains an attractive specimen.

The boy-man who snatched my virginity when I was sixteen still is recognizable. Snatched might be too strong a word, since I thought I was in love and my prize was willingly offered the night we had sex in the front seat of Stonewall's dilapidated car. That experience wasn't lovemaking, as I recall it. Maybe Stonewall's memory differs, but the experience sure wasn't pleasurable for me. Before the sex thing, Stonewall professed his love for months, telling me he wanted to marry me, but the lovey-dovey talk disappeared after we were intimate. Stonewall essentially severed our relationship a few nights after we had intercourse. He got angry because I wouldn't put out again and accused me of not being a virgin. His evidence was the bloodless hankie he gave me to wipe up with the night we had intercourse. I certainly thought I was a virgin, and I was stunned at Stonewall's accusation. It took mere seconds for me to tell him he would not touch me again, that we were finished, but it took a lot longer to get Stonewall to shut his trap and get off the front porch of my parents' farmhouse.

We certainly didn't handle our breakup well. Stonewall did a fast turnaround that last night we were together by trying to convince me he really did want to marry me, but it was too late. When he realized he wasn't making any headway, he called me a bitch for the way I was acting. My retaliation was to tell him he was a lousy lover and I hated sex with him. I made things worse by telling him my dog, Elvis, was the only one who still loved him, or maybe I said Elvis was the only one who had ever loved him. It took me years to realize how emotionally immature we were that night long ago when we stood like statutes and hurled hurtful words at each other. Stonewall was an insensitive lump of humanity, but I've never forgotten the hurt look on his face as he heard me say he had failed as a lover. I tell myself Stonewall deserved everything I said to him, but it doesn't erase my guilt. But, for cripes sake, I was sixteen years old.

I decide enough time has been spent rummaging around in past memories. I refocus on Stonewall and Freda. He appears jubilant to be rubbing against Freda. His face registers surprise after he notices me. I don't know why he is puzzled; this is my class reunion, not his. I glance away, taking another quick look around the room. There are pairs everywhere. I assume these are married couples and think it likely I will be the only person present without a spouse or a date; the thought saddens me. I don't see anyone I care to converse with, and I really am not keen on forming a threesome. The jitters are beginning to creep in again when I notice my best friend since elementary school is seated in the far right corner of the room. Hanna and her spouse, George, are busy talking to their next-seat neighbor. I get Hanna's attention before maneuvering through the crowd to reach her table.

Hugs abound. We spend an hour catching up with each other's lives, exchanging addresses and phone numbers, saying it is a shame we haven't stayed in contact, and vowing we will stay in touch forever. There is hearty laughter when we remember we were called Mutt and Jeff through the years, because she is short to my five foot, six inches. I told her she looks great. Her figure still is trim, and she looks younger than her years. She tells me I haven't changed any, a lie I appreciate.

When we were in high school, girls danced with each other, including waltzing, all which was considered perfectly normal. We probably were naïve, since we didn't have a thought about lesbians or gays, although I later learned there were some homosexuals in our crowd. When Docks plays Chubby Checker's "Let's Do the Twist," Hanna says we have to dance. I could do a mean twist when I was young, but I'm out of practice. Rodney didn't like dancing too much; he used to tell me football players thought dancing was for sissies. As I enter the dance floor, I recall being nominated for best dancer my senior year, but Molly Flanders won. Molly always beat me at everything—best dancer, cheerleader, best looking, and she always got first crack at all the jocks. I hope she will show up later. I'm eager to know how life has changed the prettiest girl in our senior class.

As soon as Hanna and I start dancing, I realize the moves have been residing in my bones all along. I still can groove. It doesn't take me long to decide I will try the crème de la crème by twisting downward until I place my hands on the floor. People clap for more, so I oblige. I notice Stonewall starring intensely, even though Freda is at his side. I wonder if they are married. If they are, it isn't stopping him from enjoying my dancing. I sex up my gyrations. While I have no interest in Stonewall, it is fun knowing I am able to generate heat. I feel pretty good about my appearance. Most of the weight I added to the 112 pounds I weighed my senior year has disappeared with the dieting and exercise I added to my routine after Rodney died. My tan complements the purple silk pant suit and white silk blouse I'm wearing. I rarely wear underwear, and the silk feels luscious against my skin. The tune ends, and I rush to get a large glass of ice water to cool down. I don't think I've been so steamed in a long time.

Hanna and I decide to get something to eat before we sit down, but the food is subpar, so we eat a few olives and chips and start back to our table. Stonewall steps in front of me and asks me to dance. With a hint of snippiness, I retort, "What about Freda?" There is anger in his voice when he replies, "We are friends—not married." I decide he must be telling the truth or Freda would have stopped him from approaching me.

Discomfort joins me as Stonewall draws me to his body, but my uneasiness promptly disappears. We still fit together well. Small talk is exchanged, as we dance to Johnny Mathis' "Chances Are." I ask Stonewall about his mother. He tells me she has been dead five years, tagging on to the end of his sentence, "You know she loved you dearly."

"I do know. She told me she loved me when she sent me a gift at graduation. She said I was the one she wanted you to marry. Did you know she contacted me?"

"No, I didn't; but I married twice, and Mom disliked both of my wives. She always was telling me I let the right one get away. I guess she was right, since my marriages ended in divorce."

"The divorces don't mean we were meant to be together, Stonewall. A marriage between us likely would have been disastrous, too."

"You can say that, Sue, but I never stopped loving you."

Stonewall's words bewildered me. I needed some distance between us, but he clutched me tighter when I tried to move away. "Let go of me, Stonewall. I want to sit down."

"Sue, please don't push me away. Can we go talk in the car?"

"I don't want any more experiences in the front seat of a car with you, Stonewall. The last one didn't turn out very well."

"I was pretty stupid then, Sue, but please give me a few minutes of your time. Please. I only want to talk. I won't touch you."

"All right, let's go talk. Getting into a car with you probably is poor judgment on my part. I swear I'll claw your eyeballs out if you touch me."

I retrieve my purse and tell Hanna and George I am leaving to talk to Stonewall. I stifle their questioning looks by saying, "Don't worry. I'll call you later at the motel. We'll talk some more." I allow Stonewall to take my hand and thread me around the people dancing. It didn't take long to reach his automobile, a new red convertible with a name unknown to me. Stonewall gripped the steering wheel as he gushed, "Sue, I never should have raised the issue about your virginity. It was none of my business, and it didn't matter anyway. Really, it didn't. Forgive me."

I feel suppressed anger surfacing again. I wonder why men expect they will be excused from every wrongdoing if the word "please" is attached to their request for forgiveness. "You are right, Stonewall, my virginity was never any of your business. If you wanted me to remain pure as snow, why didn't you keep your hands off me when we were dating? I'm sorry I didn't live up to your expectations, but, frankly, I have news for you. You didn't meet my expectations, either."

"Sue, I didn't mean—"

"Stop talking. I'm not finished. Don't feel badly. Don't apologize anymore. Turns out you probably were right about my not being a virgin, but I don't know for sure."

"What do you mean?"

"Shortly after we broke up, I started having a recurrent dream. I don't know how old I am in the dream, maybe about five. A former neighbor, a male, who was quite a few years older than me, is the other person in the dream. He and I, and another neighbor, a female, used to be playmates. One of the games we played was 'Doctor.' In my dream, we are in the basement of this boy's home, and this boy is trying to remove my panties. I'm resisting, crying, and begging him to stop. I awaken before my underwear is removed, always filled with a sense of dread, my pillow and nightclothes wet with tears. I'm always happy I've been dreaming. This dream reoccurred frequently over years."

"Did it stop?"

"I'm getting to that. Sometime after I morphed into my late thirties, I learned from the female friend I previously mentioned that she believes she was molested by this same male. We decided our memories might just be playing a cruel trick on us. Anyway, even if I could be certain the molestation happened, it's too late to confront the culprit, even if I could make contact with him. The truth is it's too late for me to disrupt my life and the lives of others. The good thing is that after talking with this person from my past, my recurrent dream ceased. I've made my peace with the painful memory as best I can. All I've just told you does not change the fact I thought I was a virgin when we coupled. I'm sorry, Stonewall, but I don't think I'm capable of forgiving you."

Stonewall moaned, "I'm truly sorry, Sue. Give me a chance to make it up to you."

Probably thinking he could take me in his arms and comfort me, Stonewall moved toward me. I recoiled, stiffened my arms and flung them into the space between us. "Don't. Don't you dare touch me. You promised. The past can't be changed. If I was molested, it can't be reversed. I don't want to talk about any of it anymore. Nothing is going to change."

"Sue, I—"

"Stonewall, the bad things that happened to us in the past, the sex and all, can't be erased, either. I'm sorry I said mean things to you the last night we were together, but you doomed our relationship the instant you raised the virginity issue. I don't want to talk about it anymore. Shit happens."

"I don't want to dwell on the past any more than you do, Sue, but I love you. I want you in my life."

"Stop it, Stonewall. It isn't going to happen. I'm a different person now. I don't know what I'll want in the future in terms of male companionship, but what I know I don't want is a male who hurt me deeply because of his warped ego or his sense of entitlement."

"You won't forgive me"?

"There is nothing to forgive. As I told you before, you probably were right. The problem is you wounded me deeply by questioning my virginity. It was a stinking, rotten thing for you to do! I'm glad we had this conversation, and I'm delighted you are doing well, but we are not going to be a couple again. Ever! Do you get it?"

"Sue, give me a chance. Love conquers all."

"You sound like a dopey teenager, Stonewall. Enough of this sad-sack stuff. Why don't you do something that will give us both pleasure? Put the top down on this baby and take us for a ride! You can cruise me to Tazewell and Richlands and drive me through every street in the two Bluefields. Maybe we can find at least one restaurant open that serves decent food. You have to promise me first that you won't talk anymore about love. You promise?"

Moment of the Deer

Olivia Stowe

"You know, the chocolate disks covered with gold foil."

"We don't have those."

"You know, the ones made up like gold coins; they have them every Christmas."

"It's Christmas Eve. We sold out on those more than a week ago."

"I mean my son decided the family could come tomorrow after all at the last minute, and we have those for the grandchildren every year they visit. Well, might you know where I could—?"

"No, I don't," Nancy cut in, anxious to move the line along. "We sold out of those last week." She had, in fact, seen those a day or two before over at CVS, but there was no reason why she should be sending business over there. There was no reason why she should have to work on Christmas Eve at all. People could jolly well think ahead on their needs.

The man just sort of zoned out of her attention. Her gaze had been arrested by an elderly women, with scraggly gray hair and in what looked like an overcoat over a nightgown and scruffy slippers, wandering around in aisle two. When Nancy looked back across the cash register, the man looking for the chocolate coins was gone, to be replaced by a weary-looking young woman with a baby in her arms and a fat toddler pulling at her leg. The woman had put a can of infant formula on the conveyer belt and was rummaging around in her purse, saying she thought she had a store coupon for that. Her toddler had his chubby hand in a can of candy canes on the counter and had pulled one out.

"Should he be doing that?" Nancy asked sharply, an edge to her voice. The nerve of some people loading their fat kids up on candy, she thought. She really didn't approve of the store putting out things out there to tempt the brats anyway.

"Oh, sorry," the woman said. "Well, all right, Mikey," she went on to say to the toddler. "But just because it's Christmas."

"Excuse me," a rather dreamy, confused voice drifted into Nancy's hearing as she was finishing ringing the young woman up. "Can you tell me where the Tums are? I can't seem to find them, and my Ralph is—"

"Right over there on aisle three," Nancy said with a bit of exasperation in her voice to the old woman in the overcoat. "Right where they've always been," she muttered sotto voce as the elderly woman drifted away.

The shift from hell, Nancy thought. She was glad when this one would be over. She hadn't really had any plans for Christmas Eve, but no one should have to work an evening shift on this day.

At last the shift was over, but Nancy's irritation increased as she was driving home and found she had to detour around the main street between her work and her apartment because they had a drive-by Christmas lights display along that stretch of the road. She hadn't thought about that being there and had reached a point where she'd have to take a winding, rural road around the town or backtrack to get to the highway going through on the other side of the town.

She turned onto the rural road and sped up a little faster than she should to make up for the lost time the detour would cause.

She rounded a curve and went into shock as the headlights picked up a large deer standing still in the middle of the road. Deer and woman froze, panicked eyes latched onto panicked eyes. And, as the deer leaped in one direction, Nancy's car lurched in the other direction, and she went down into a ditch and up into a tree, the tail of car still on the apron of the road.

She sat there, dazed from having her head bounce off the side window. The hit wasn't hard enough to set off her airbag, but she saw stars and felt the ooze of blood at her temple.

She was bathed in the headlights of another car, and a man and woman, dressed in evening apparel, appeared at the side of the car, almost instantly, giving her very concerned looks as she rolled the window down.

"Are you all right?" the man asked?

"Are you hurt?" the woman chimed in.

"A deer. It was a deer," Nancy said, rather dumbly.

But right at that moment the beam from a strong flashlight appeared at the corner of the passenger side of Nancy's car, revealing that she'd gone off the edge of the road right next to a driveway.

"I heard the crash," a man was calling out. "Anyone hurt? Oh, that doesn't look too good. Here, let me help you up to the house and we'll see about that gash . . . and about your car. It'll have to be moved or there'll be another crash here."

"I'll stay with her car until a wrecker comes," the first man said.

"I'll go call the Mitchells on my cell phone and tell them we'll be late to the party," his wife called out as she started back to their car. "We'd better leave our headlights shining on her car until the wrecker gets here so anyone else coming around the curve can see it in time."

As the man whose driveway Nancy plowed across and who identified himself as Steve Brandon helped her up to his house, he was asking her if she was in pain anywhere else, but she said she didn't think so. "Still, we'd best call Doc Watson— they live a couple of driveways down—and ask him if he can come over and take a look at you. Do you have AAA?"

"Eh, no, no, I'm sorry, I don't," Nancy answered. She was still feeling a little woozy.

"Guess I'll call Joe Timberman then," Steve said. "He's got the Exxon station up on Maple. Maybe he can bring his truck over and take your car over there at least for tonight. When that's taken care of, I'll drive you home."

When they entered the house, Steve's wife was there, looking concerned and putting her arms around Nancy and helping her to a chair between the fireplace, where a fire was flickering, and a lighted Christmas tree. It was clear that Steve had been assembling toys for young children hopefully abed and at least pretending to be asleep in anticipation of Christmas morning.

"Oh, you can't drive me home. You're—" Nancy muttered.

"I was figuring I'd be up half the night getting this together anyway," Steve said with a laugh. "Another hour or two won't matter much."

"Here, dear," Steve's wife said as she returned from the kitchen. "Here is a mug of hot chocolate and a few Christmas cookies. I called Doc Watson. He was at his daughter's house, but he said he'd be over within a half hour. I'll go call Joe Timberman now."

* * * *

"It looks worse than it is," Doc Watson said as he finished cleaning the gash on Nancy's temple. "A butterfly bandage should do for now. But maybe you should go into the hospital in the morning to get that checked out. I can meet you there and help you through the process, if you like."

"But it's Christmas tomorrow," Nancy said in a near whisper.

"People need help on Christmas Day as much as any other," Doc Watson answered. "It's all in what folks do for other folks."

Nancy was murmuring her thanks as she heard the sounds of activity out on the road. She stood and went to the window and saw that a wrecker had arrived and two men were hooking up the tail end of her car to a hoist. The couple in the evening apparel were still there, with the headlights of their car beamed on hers.

Movement caught Nancy's attention out of the corner of her eye, and she turned her gaze to where, bathed in moonlight and standing in a majestic stance in a clearing at the edge of the forest—and peering straight into her face—was a deer. Perhaps the same deer she'd already encountered.

They were both frozen there for a long moment, eyes latched onto eyes. Nancy's eyes teared up, though, in sudden recognition that something had touched her deeply inside on this Christmas Eve. When she had cleared the haze of her vision, the deer had disappeared.

90

POETRY

Herculaneum

Lori Magai Dixon

When the sun obscured, and ash began to fall
Did they beg the gods' deliverance, berate
Each other's little sins, wail that the world
Would end and everything was lost?
Or did they hide their heads from burning rain
Lie down in one another's arms, perhaps
Make a shield of a shawl or coat, and hold it
So their final sight was one another's face?
This much is sure, the bones that lie in last embrace
Defying—not death, which will always come—but
Despair, which need not visit, not even at the end of
things,
Affirm, both in their bodies' pose and tender
Hand in bony hand, that love endures, is strong enough
And will outlast, as long as bones remain.

Radishes and Roses Café

Marilou Schunter

(Honorable Mention poetry, Writer's Eye contest, 2013, inspired by Ankerre (Emu), 1990, Emily Kame Kngwarrey, viewable at http://www.virginia.edu/artmuseum/pdf/WE2013/selections_adult.pdf)

after the glittery ivory trails
of our daughter's wedding gown
have been swept up into her car
we dance in red autumn meadow
soon swallowed by rainstorm
revelers retreat under tents
crowd round white tables
to nibble on sponge cake
quaff golden champagne
afterwards we gather bouquets
tied with ribbon to take home
where we kick off our shoes
devour chicken salad croissants
ordered for Sunday brunch
in the morning
we request more sandwiches
but our caterer is closed
we will have to survive
on what remains

Poppies in the Dining Room

Marilou Schunter

(Honorable Mention poetry, Blue Ridge Writers VWC, 2013)

introduce a wild element
with their hairy stems
protruding from cut-glass vase
poppies are party girls
luminescent
in red and yellow petal skirts
brought in from the farm
not the hothouse
their sex appeal
overwhelms timid carnations
throws everything off-kilter
bright stamen crowns
tickle my fancy
remind me of the days
we made love everywhere

Night Moths

Sigrid Mirabella

(Second place poetry, Blue Ridge Writers VWC, 2013)

She's very still on the laid pine,
naked and splayed to the floor,
flush upon furry black rug.
She looks pale as a humid moon,
her lips licked soft and parted
in the way a question is thought
yet not expressed. How many
blonde strands spidering her shoulders,
flayed across pulsed breast, witness
love hurry to take her mouth,
press hard muscle to soft?

She moves one hand to his nape,
lightly fingers damp brown curls,
her nose against his chest inhales
with his exhales, pulls his aroma
to her heart. Heat sweats into beads,
slips from one body to other.

The cat perched quiet on sill,
turns towards them a moment
then goes back to watching insects
outside the window. The sound of two as one,
the sound of river birth, equilibrium
in the universe, numbers unhinged from logic,
a cat's paw against glass swatting night moths.

Pop-Eye

David Black

(Third place poetry, Blue Ridge Writers VWC, 2013)

For just a minute all four feet
stopped and he was suspended
just above the ground, but that was later,
after Ogden had rescued this one-eyed mutt,
fed him, treated his mange
with motor oil and sulphur,
tried to get him to hunt
only to find out he wouldn't,

and it was just after
he ran up on Dad and me
when we were on a deer stand,
and just before all four feet
and the rest of him hit the ground
after Dad caught him
in mid-stride with a load of #4 shot.

The Master's Touch

Jack Trammell

(Honorable Mention poetry, Blue Ridge Writers VWC, 2013)

Be mindful.

Light, carefree, arm-hair zephyrs . . .

Pay attention.

Pause before turning the next page,
Savor the very last word in the paragraph   (*clouds.*)

Thought *is* prayer,
The More in transition
To the blue sky hope of
New mothers and introspective old men
Glad for the sunshine.

Silence sings away fear,
Proof of uncertainty in
Musical notes that merge
Into a surf's crashing symphony
Someone else's prayer surreptitiously overheard.

Pray not to be healed, but to
Feel the light breeze, again
To notice the wayward journey a
Feeling makes coming and going along
A narrow country road just discovered.

A left turn into the kiss of the wind;
The master's touch.

Now . . .

Turn the page.

an essence in being

Marvin Loyd Welborn

(Honorable Mention poetry, Blue Ridge Writers VWC, 2013)

I hope I become
  some part
of memory

somewhere
  of someone
a snapshot of mind

an image
  a record
a minuscule sign

I too then
  shall last
beyond
  my just measure

a slit so affixed
  a fitted
assigned

no name,
  need remember
no facts,
  there attached

just an image
  of me
of some kind

when gone
  I will still

somehow engender

what more
  can one ask
from all time?

Lovers

Cornelia Clay Fulghum

What would console you,
She asked him in a pensive frame of mind,
As she artfully inclined
In his direction.

If you knew for sure
My love would never fade,
In some terrible cascade
Of anguished grief and guilt?

If you could ascertain
That God exists,
And that life persists
After the body fails?

Or if you were able
To see through illusion—
This perfusion
Of sorrows
And horrors
On our earth—to know
They are a passing show,
That underneath is universal order,
Despite unending slaughter
Of men and beasts?

Tell me, would you then be comforted
And feel a lasting peace?

He smiled, but did not speak.
How can I say to her, he wondered,
That peace will only come
When I'm content
To watch her beauty wane,

To let the world
Disintegrate around me,
My arms spread wide,
Aware, that nothing tangible

Will abide?

He thought: Perhaps it is uncivilized and uncouth
To say to her, We are all
Forever
In free fall,
But it's the truth.
And isn't truth the only consolation?

Can I say: When I am brave enough
Not to wish for anything
But to exist
In this astonishing,
Precipitous present,
Then it is
That I feel peace
And even bliss?

Can I tell her,
This?

Roses Remember

Elizabeth Doyle Solomon

Soft rain crept down on cushioned feet
late last evening, fresh and sweet—
opened buds on wild roses' hedge,
petal-pink-falls over the edge—

just like the roses which greeted me
coming home each night so sleepily—
tumbling over Llanarth's entry way
where June's full moon shone her silvered ray.

How hard those years, two hours' commute,
this love for teaching firm, resolute—
each summer, camp kids flocked to my farm,
small nature lovers brought their own charm.

We combed and we roamed the farm's deep woods,
each day exploring their precious goods—
touching and smelling ev'ry flower wild,
wonder too, in the eyes of each child.

I know they remember just as I,
roses beneath Llanarth's summer sky—
rain frogs and thrushes, owls at night,
memories cherished, beautiful-bright.

I Hit a Deer

Gary D. Kessler

I hit a deer today.
Or rather the deer hit me.

Were you hurt?
the friends asked.
Did it total the car?

No, I'm OK,
At least in that way.

But, no, that's a lie;
I watched a doe die.

I know it wasn't my fault
I stopped, hoping she could vault.

I sat with her to the end, eye to eye
Knowing she was asking why she had to die.

Her life simple, trusting, unknowing of the world of
man,
Just roaming the wood, caring for her fawn her only
plan.

Good you weren't hurt,
said well-meaning friends.
And the car will mend.

Yes, but.
Yes . . . but.

I killed a deer today,
and it's not the car that most needs to mend.

Lost . . . and Found

Phyllis R. Koch-Sheras

I lost my friend Joe last night—
The same date I lost my father 27 years ago;
I lost Hollie, my precious 16-year old Retriever last month;
And I lost my favorite watch today;

I go to walk our little Lasa Apso, Tigle, at our familiar terrain;
It doesn't feel the same without Hollie bounding off at every turn;
I look to see where she went—
No place now that I can find her—
Except in my heart.

While walking, I call Phylicia on the cell phone:
When will the memorial service for her husband Joe be held?
We both say, "I can't believe it."
It is on my way home that I notice my watch is not on my wrist;
I retrace my steps twice to no avail;
I feel a wave of sadness and despair;
My watch, my dog, my father, my friend—
All just disappear as if in a fog.

You were my companions and support for so many years,
And now you're gone—like time itself,
Existing only moment to moment—impermanent;
Perhaps we only notice the pain when the ones we love are gone,
Only fully appreciate them when they have passed on;
Gone but not forgotten;
Out of sight, but not out of mind.
Being with you all enriched my life;
Let it be—
Lost and found in eternity.

Yet Another Massacre

Sarah Collins Honenberger

Like the drunk
he hurtles into the silent night
misunderstood, befuddled,
alone with his anger at a world
he blames for what
he cannot control.
He shoulders the destruction
as if it were
a returning hero's medal,
held proudly
to flash in the sun.
Aiming at nothing and everything,
he drives into that black void,
spewing havoc and hate
like gravel in his wake.

And like the drunk,
he wakes alone, bleeding inside,
inert and unaware
that behind him lies a mangled truth,
a loss, a devastation,
so wide
no human hand can heal,
no human heart can bridge
nor comprehend.
Only the featherweight hand of God
held to his trembling child,
and whispers of what might have been
if love were everything,
instead of only a rare sighting
at dawn.

PROSE NONFICTION

The Most Fragile Gift

Susan M. Lanterman

It's the call that can stop a parent's heart. "There's been a terrible accident," our pastor explained. "An eighteen-year-old boy is in critical condition at the medical center. Can the mom stay at your inn?"

The next evening Ce Ce arrived. She desired only a night's rest before returning to her bedside vigil. She was a tiny woman with wispy blonde hair and pixie blue eyes framed in mascara—now smudged with fatigue and worry. "They told me when they flew Chandler over the mountain . . ." she paused to gain composure. ". . . that he wouldn't survive. I told them I wasn't leaving his side," she said, her voice weak but determined.

Several days of pounding rain had converted potholes into shallow troughs on the rural road he had traveled through Rockingham County. On a brisk, clear day, Chandler's car hydroplaned into a tree, wrapping around it like a crushed soda can. "He had a stroke and has been in a coma ever since," Ce Ce sobbed, her eyes fluttering with tears. She had just graduated from nursing school and knew too well the severity of his injuries and the probable outcome.

She settled into a routine of sharing late-night progress reports and early-morning coffees before trekking over to the Neuro ICU at the University of Virginia. Days turned into weeks. The hospital staff bolstered her resolve to remain positive. She began each morning reading Psalm 30 to her boy: *"I cried to you for help, and you restored my health. You brought me up from the grave, O Lord, and kept me from falling into the pit of death . . ."* Chandler lay beneath her careful watch, rigid and unresponsive. She continued to fill the air with her voice, singing old hymns and reciting familiar childhood stories. On the weekends, extended family gathered around the bed, attempting to stimulate Chandler with one-sided conversations.

Ce Ce's family asked what they could give us in return for hosting her. Chandler's recovery was our only desire. Then, one weekend an unexpected gift came. "You have a Bed and

Breakfast and we have eggs!" The family homestead was located next to a poultry farm. We couldn't refuse.

Like the "Twelve Days of Christmas," we received deliveries amounting to twelve dozen double yolkers on our doorstep. Then an unexpected snowstorm hit, crippling Charlottesville. The phone rang—it was our pastor again. "This was supposed to be our last day hosting the homeless but now that the road is closed we have forty hungry men stranded due to the storm. Is it possible to bring over whatever food you can spare?" We lived only one block from the church. I thought— eggs. We have eggs enough to feed a multitude. We made a variety of quiches and plowed through the snow to the church.

Back at the inn, Ce Ce laughed when she heard we could *pay it forward*—feeding the homeless with eggs. Then, her momentary elation flickered back to a simmer, her thoughts retreated to her son lying in a hospital bed, surrounded by a halo of wires.

"What a miracle it would be if Chandler came out of his coma," she thought aloud.

In the fourth week of Chandler's deep sleep, just before Christmas, he raised two fingers to form a "V". The nurses joined the hallelujah chorus sung by his friends and family. He continued to improve incrementally, and by New Years he had regained memory, the sight in one eye, and his ability to communicate. Doctors said it would take years of therapy and a tremendous amount of courage to return to the carefree world in which he once lived. The stroke had temporarily robbed him of his handsome smile and his ability to control one side of his body, but he was undeterred. Despite the risk of losing his eye, he asked for the eyelid on his wounded face to be released from its "permanent stitches." He fought to regain normalcy, one wobbly step at a time.

Mother and child continue to venture over the mountain to stay at our inn when Chandler has medical appointments at the hospital. With a crooked grin and a guarded gait, Ce Ce's boy jokes about his lack of balance. His injury will prohibit him from ever walking a straight line again. He also comes to Charlottesville to comfort families who have kids in comas in the ICU. Ce Ce pats Chandler's arm proudly as he prepares to speak to the UVa Residents and ER staff. They call him their Christmas Miracle.

Ce Ce and her son remind us how quickly a life can be shattered. And yet how a tragedy can be a catalyst for positive change in someone else's life. Through much effort, Chandler has resumed the life of the young man who was driving that rainy day—he is working, attending school and living independently.

An ornament hangs in my kitchen commemorating a fragile life saved and a life giving back. A blue crystal egg, from Ce Ce.

Taking the Waters

Jean Lancaster

(Second place nonfiction, Virginia Writers Club Summer Shorts, 2013)

My father often told a story about how he and his two brothers, when youngsters in the 1920s, would sneak into the Warm Springs women's bathhouse in the middle of the night. The circular building had an opening low on one side where the water flowed from the spring-fed pool into the stream. The excursion must have been much like swimming into a water-filled, dark cave.

My uncles selected my father, who was the youngest, to swim through the gap in the boards. He popped up in the overflow room, where there was a powerful waterfall rushing from the pool. This served as a massage treatment for infirm visitors who would be lowered in a chair on ropes and pulleys. From there, my father climbed the slippery stairs to the pool deck and opened a window in one of the dressing rooms. His brothers crawled through into the closet-sized space, and they all shed their pajamas. The boys spent the quiet night hours floating in the water and watching the stars twinkle through the skylight in the domed roof.

When my father's mother was a young woman, Nana and her sisters lived in the Warm Springs Hotel's Gibson Cottage that was on a hill just above the bathhouses. They walked down the lane after breakfast every day to "take the waters" in the Ladies Pool House that was built in 1836.

The weathered, walnut-colored face of the attendant would greet the sisters as they entered. She had worked at the bathhouse her whole life, just as her mother and grandmother had throughout their lives. She handed each of them a freshly laundered white towel and a flower-print, cotton bathing suit. Large buttons secured each shoulder and long, loose legs covered the knees.

Nana navigated the circular wooden deck to a dressing room and pulled the curtain closed behind her. Thin, yellowed fabric billowed out toward the pool, fluttered by the breeze that blew through the gaps between the wallboards and around the window frame. She hung her clothes on a peg and walked back out onto the narrow deck. She smiled a sly grin as she walked down the half-dozen wooden steps into the water and settled her feet on the stone-lined bottom.

She never wore one of those feed sack outfits, never once in her life. She bathed in just the skin she was born in. Nana believed that the mineral waters nourished her body with nutrients from deep in the earth and cleansed her soul just like a bedtime prayer.

After soaking for an hour or more, Nana and her sisters would sit awhile outside on a bench in the gazebo. The Drinking Spring between the men's and women's bathhouses ascended into a crystal clear stream. In a communion-like ritual, they sipped the sulfur-infused water from the metal dipper that hung on a nail. When my siblings and I were children, we sipped the same warm water from the long-handled ladle and held our noses to keep from breathing in the rotten-egg odor.

Throughout their fifty-year marriage, my father and mother spent a week each summer at the Warm Springs Inn to "take the waters" daily. After our mother passed away, my sister, brother, and I took our elderly father back to that nostalgic retreat. My brother held Dad's arm on the way to the octagonal Gentlemen's Pool House that has stood there since 1761. Once inside, though, my father insisted on entering the pool on his own, holding the stair railings, his body recovering its youthfulness with each step into that fabled water.

An early legend recounted the discovery of the springs by a young American Indian who was weary from his journey across the Allegheny Mountains. He carried "a message from his powerful tribe to the council fire kindling on the shore of the Great Water." He saw the reflection of a star in a spring in the valley, and "the warm vapor that rose to his nostrils tempted him into the pool so that he might bathe his aching limbs." Lying down in the waters, "the Spirit of Strength gave him new life and hope."

Later, in 1806, a visitor to Warm Springs recorded that there were "log huts; the smell of the copious spring; fifty-to-sixty people with attendant servants, horses, and carriages; one man who slept in the springs at night; and a near drowning." In 1846 physician William Burke wrote *The Mineral Springs of Western Virginia*. He noted that "after a few bathings in the Warm Springs, gout and rheumatic cripples begin to exercise those joints where immoveable . . . and soon enjoy entire exemption from pain." Dr. John Brockenbrough, proprietor of the property at that time, built a wing on the Gentlemen's Pool House that contained "a cold plunging bath, which is plentifully supplied with spring water from the neighboring hills."

While the mineral waters are invigorating, they are also enervating. When some Tennessee soldiers passed through Bath County during the Civil War, they "all went down there and went in, it felt so good, that some of the fellows stayed so long that when they got out they were so weak they could hardly walk."

After decades of ownership by private owners, the Homestead Resort obtained the property and renamed it the Jefferson Pools in honor of the famous Virginian's visit there in 1818. A volunteer group, The Friends of Warm Springs Pools, is working diligently to save "the oldest spa structures in the United States" and to preserve the memories of "taking the waters." The Warm Springs Bathhouses are listed on both the Virginia Landmarks Register and The National Register of Historic Places. Preservation Virginia nominated the pools to its "2010 Most Endangered Historic Sites in Virginia."

For the past five years my sister, two friends, and I have made our pilgrimage during the first weekend in December. Each year, we have been blissfully snowed in at the Inn at Gristmill Square. We "take the waters" every day. When the attendant offers the bathing suit, I tell her, "No thank you, I will bathe in just the skin I was born in."

I immerse my shoulders under the water amidst the prism patterns reflecting on the clear surface. Snowflakes drift down through the now cracked and missing panes of the domed skylight. The 98-degree water is soothing and reminds me of the salty waters of the ocean. Steam rises throughout like a hot-stone sauna. Swarms of bubbles, pushed up by the earth's gases, drift up from the stone-lined bottom to tickle my skin. The mineral-rich water draws impurities and anxieties out from deep within me.

The pool is quiet with usually less than a half-dozen women there in the winter. My close-knit group floats silently in meditation. Sometimes, though, we whisper together about sneaking in at night, but we are never been brave enough to attempt this mystical journey.

The African Queen

(Second place nonfiction, Blue Ridge Writers VWC, 2013)

The examining room door cracked open just enough to accommodate a seemingly disembodied smiling face and balding head.

"The African Queen, I presume!"

"Shut up, Alan. It's bad enough sitting here in this demoralizing paper rag without you making fun of me."

Dr. Stein, longtime doctor and family friend, chuckled as he picked up my chart.

"Why an African safari, Lucinda?"

"Well, I was leafing through *Architectural Digest* and saw this ad: 'Come to Nairobi, sit in the Thorn Tree Café, sip a glass of chardonnay, and watch the world go by.' It was sort of a divorce present to myself. I sent in my deposit and outfitted myself with a new camera."

"So, why are you here, Lucinda?"

"Take your pick—a cold, severe sunburn, diarrhea, a limp . . ."

* * * *

When I boarded the plane, much to my delight, the two other seats in my row were empty. I settled myself into the seat by the window and fastened my seatbelt. I breathed a sigh of relief when the plane took off and reached cruising altitude. Then I unclenched my fingers from the armrests. Flying was not my favorite thing. After dinner I put my seat back and closed my eyes. I was just dozing off when I heard a commotion six seats in front of me.

"I'm not drunk," the fat man hiccupped.

"You lush, get away from me," shouted the carrot-headed woman next to him.

116

To my horror he wobbled down the aisle and sat down in my row on the far seat. The middle seat was all that remained between me and the stench of scotch. I shut my eyes as he ordered another drink from the tight-lipped stewardess. In the next several hours he drank five more scotches and watched me try to sleep. At 3:00 a.m. we landed in Dublin, Ireland, to refuel. We disembarked, and I went to the bar and ordered Irish coffee. When we took off again I was happy to see that *my friend* sat back down beside his lady.

As we approached Nairobi, the sky began to lighten. The stars dimmed and faded in a blur of pastels, the color palette of an impressionistic painting brushed with peach and pink and lavender. In the distance, through some wispy clouds, I could see an amazing triple rainbow over Mt. Kilimanjaro.

We were met at the airport by our tour guide, Julie. She escorted us by bus to our hotel, where she delivered her orientation talk. Afterward I went to my assigned room to rest before we regrouped in the lobby and were driven to a local market. It was crowded and hot. The panoply of fruit, meat, fish, and vegetables of every imaginable size, shape, and color was unreal. Farm animals, chickens, goats, and calves were evident, if not by sight, certainly by smell. There were tables of beautiful, naturally dyed fabrics. The native vendors' constant chatter droned in the air, and it was difficult, if not impossible, to understand the various dialects. The market was pulsing with activity, and serious negotiations about price were a constant, but generally were agreed upon sooner or later.

Back at the hotel I dressed for dinner and, over cocktails, mingled with some of the guests. Julie, our guide, walked by and put her hand on my shoulder.

"Hi, Lucinda, how's everything?"

"Great," I said.

"I'd like to introduce you to some really nice people."

I followed her through the crowded lounge. That's how I met Gigi, John, Stu, and Frank.

"Guys, this is Lucinda, the lady I was telling you about. I thought that, since you're all singles, you might like to travel in the bush together."

This suited us all fine, and thus was formed a very congenial fivesome. After breakfast the next morning we were bused to our jeep and driver some thirty minutes away. Our driver's name was Saba. His jeep looked as if it had seen better days, but after coughing a few times, it chugged slowly along. Finally, we reached a vast, open plain.

"Be quiet and look to left," Saba instructed.

Not three hundred feet away were two adult giraffes. They kept circling each other, their necks intertwining.

"This is giraffe, how you say . . . foreplay," Saba said.

"Foreplay," laughed John.

"Shh," Saba hissed.

After about twenty minutes of watching this strange courtship, nothing progressed further, and, with great disappointment and reluctance, we drove on. Soon we spotted a small herd of zebras, and we frantically began snapping pictures. I guess we thought maybe these were the last zebras we were ever going to see.

"No stripes like any other zebra," said Saba. "All different, you know . . . unique."

"Like us," I quipped.

Over the next several days we saw warthogs, rhinos, springbok, impalas, lions, and elephants. While we were following the large family of elephants, a big bull bringing up the rear suddenly turned and charged our jeep. We were out of there in a hurry.

The third day out we were waved down by a bare-chested native. He ran beside our jeep wildly waving his arms and yelling. We were able to make out, "Crazy lion . . .run amok . . . kill somebody." Saba accelerated, but the jeep refused to budge. To my amazement Stu jumped out and managed to patch something under the hood up with some wire from Gigi's steno pad. Back at the lodge, in the local paper we read that two people had been killed by a crazed renegade lion.

Later that evening, on a four-foot-high terrace overlooking a nearby watering hole, under a star-filled sky, in the middle of nowhere, we were served an elegant dinner prepared by French-trained chefs. The night was warm, and a pleasant breeze wafted through the soft, humid air. Sounds of wild animals and jungle insects orchestrated an exotic background concert. Several species came to drink.

"This is so unbelievably beautiful," Gigi murmured.

"I feel like I'm on a movie set," I replied.

"Yep, this is pretty fantastic," Frank added.

Just then we heard tree limbs being pushed apart. A huge elephant walked purposefully toward the watering hole. He didn't stop to drink, but continued toward us until he rested one humongous foot on the four-foot stone wall around the terraced dining area. Without a word everyone got up and began backing away. We all stood huddled together at the far end of the terrace. Two armed native guards with rifles appeared. The elephant trumpeted loudly, lowered his foot, and nonchalantly walked away, disappearing among the trees. We collectively sighed with relief, sat back down, and had tea and dessert.

Soon afterward Julie came by.

"Would you guys be willing to sleep outside in a tent tonight?"

"Why in a tent?" John asked.

"Well, it seems that the Tanzanian border has been closed because of some incident, and that means all the lodges are overcrowded and several tour groups cannot go into Tanzania. If you all agree to sleep in a tent, I'll arrange a special treat for you for you tomorrow."

Stu laughed and said, "What the heck."

We didn't get much sleep that night but had a hilarious time telling jokes and ghost stories. The next morning after outdoor showers in a shed, we boarded a big yellow bus with a driver and two uniformed guards who carried what looked like machine guns. We drove through a dense bamboo forest, listening to the shoots slam into the windows, which we had been told to keep closed. Forty-five minutes later we came to a clearing.

The doors swung open and we filed out of the bus and stood there looking at a large hut-like structure on twenty-foot stilts. We walked up a steep rope bridge past a monkey sitting on a rope railing eating a banana. That was our welcome to Snow Lake Lodge.

Once inside we were asked to sign a guest list and to indicate what animal we wished to be awakened for during the night. I thought I heard John say "Rachel Welch." The allure of the lodge was the possibility of seeing rare snow leopards come to the watering hole down below to drink. "Wake me for snow leopards," I scribbled. Gigi and I were shown to a room the size of a closet.

"This is our room?" I complained.

"So it ain't the Plaza," Gigi replied.

It looked like we would spend the night sleeping on two narrow cots in our sweaty clothes and hiking boots. But now it was time to wash up as best we could, and go meet the others on the balcony overlooking (what else) the watering hole. Once on the balcony with the others Gigi and I excused ourselves to go to the ladies room. I was washing my hands when I heard a loud shriek from her stall.

"What's the matter? Are you OK?"

"Oh my God," Gigi screamed. "I have a tick in my vagina!"

"A tick where," I yelled back.

"IN MY VAGINA!"

Truthfully, all I could think of was the old joke about the two guys fishing. One gets bitten on his penis by a poisonous snake. "Help, I'm gonna die unless the poison is sucked out," The other man shrugs his shoulders and begins to walk away. "You're right, you're gonna die."

"Help me, help me," cried Gigi, who was now really hysterical.

"Wait," I said. "One of those men on the balcony, the tall one with the black beard, is Doctor Somebody. I'll go get him."

"Hurry, please hurry," Gigi sobbed.

Out on the balcony I found Doctor What's-his-name. He had a nice smile and soft brown eyes.

"Are you a doctor?"

"Yes," he replied,

"Well, er, there's a little problem. You know Gigi, the blonde lady?"

"Yes."

"She's in the ladies room."

"Yes?"

"Well, ugh, well . . . she has ugh tick, you know, er . . . down below, and can't get it out."

"No problem," he said and walked off in the direction of the ladies room.

Five minutes later a smiling Gigi and the good doctor returned.

"By the way," Gigi asked. "What kind of doctor are you?"

"A psychotherapist," he replied.

* * * *

The next day we stayed at a beautiful lodge at Mombasa on the Indian Ocean. We ate a wonderful lunch under a blue tent with a view of the sea.

"Let's all meet at the pool after lunch," Frank said.

"I'm not going to a pool. I want to go into the Indian Ocean," I countered.

Frank, always eager to please, said he'd meet me down at the beach. After changing into my bathing suit, I joined Frank at the beach. He was already swimming, and when I timidly tiptoed into the cold water, he shouted, "Come on, don't be a chicken." I took another step up to my calves, and the worst pain I'd had ever experienced shot up my leg. In an instant it radiated throughout my body. I screamed. Frank ran out of the water and caught me as I was about to collapse.

It was a bit of a blur from that point. Two employees from the lodge scooped me up into a beach chair and carried me up the steps. Frank covered me with a beach towel. I was jostled into a maroon-colored Rolls Royce. I'm still not sure whose car it was, but I assumed it belonged to someone from the lodge. Frank climbed into the backseat with me, and we were whisked off to Mombasa Hospital. I had never experienced such pain. It felt as if my whole body was on fire. A constant stream of tears ran down my cheeks.

I was taken to a room that overlooked the Indian Ocean. A very compassionate English nurse put my foot into what felt like a pail of boiling water. Across the narrow hallway newborn babies were being brought to their mothers for feeding. I remember thinking I should have one of those babies as a reward for all this pain.

There was bad news . . . and good news. I had been bitten by a stonefish. Yes, it was poisonous! Good news . . . you didn't die. More bad news . . . the doctor was out in the bush (what the hell does that mean anyway?), and I would have to wait for him to return. It seemed the nurse, maybe she wasn't, was not permitted to administer the necessary injections. Dying began to sound like a reasonable option.

> *My ashes hurled to the wind over the Indian Ocean, dancing for a moment on the white-capped waves, before they sank slowly into the azure water . . . my family, who had traveled thousands of miles stood sobbing on the sandy shore.*

I hastily reconsidered. Dying in Mombasa was just too absurd. About two hours later the doctor arrived. The pain had gradually begun to subside, but I did wonder what degree burns I had on my foot from the boiling water. He gave me two antihistamine injections. Soon I felt considerably better, although wiped out from the ordeal. The doctor wanted me to stay in the hospital overnight. I began to cry again. Finally, he said if someone would stay with me that night he would release me. Frank immediately volunteered.

Back at the lodge Frank moved my stuff into his room. I was limping badly and knocked out from the drugs. He put me and my pajamas in the bathroom and said to yell when I was ready. He came to get me and helped me into one of the single beds. He sat on the edge and took my hand.

"If you touch me, I'm going to scream."

"Take it easy. I'm not doing anything. Go to sleep."

He leaned over and kissed my forehead. I realized how ridiculous I sounded.

"Good night, Frank. Thank you."

* * * *

122

Let me tell you about Frank. He really was this genuinely nice guy from New Jersey. He carried my gear for the remainder of the trip, was totally solicitous, and was a complete gentleman. Suffice to say, for me, the romantic chemistry was just not there.

Too soon we were back in Nairobi, tanning our bodies on the roof of our hotel. We wanted to look healthy and rested for our last night in Nairobi, where we were being taken to a casino for a farewell dinner and a bit of gambling. By dinnertime my laundry list of ailments was as follows: I looked like "leather lady" from too much sun and had a blossoming cold, headache, diarrhea, and a pronounced limp.

About sixteen of us sat at a long table. At no time were we all present. There was a constant parade headed for, or coming back from, the restrooms. Everyone was afraid to drink any wine because of stomach problems, and we picked at our food because we were afraid to eat. After dinner, in the casino, Frank deposited me at a blackjack table and went to play the slots. An extremely attractive, well-dressed Indian man was seated next to me. He introduced himself, lit my cigarettes with his gold lighter, and glanced often at his large diamond-faced watch. I was flattered by the attention and flirtatious banter. An hour or so later Frank came to tell me our bus was waiting. My new friend asked that I stay, that his car and driver would see me back to my hotel. It took me only a few seconds to say thanks, but no thanks. Enough was enough. I had survived wild animals, ticks, a stonefish bite, severe sunburn, a headache, and a cold. I thanked him and said goodnight.

Back in Manhattan, I crept into my bed. The next morning I made an appointment to visit my longtime family doctor and get checked out. A few hours later, sitting on the examining table in those awful paper robes, I could hear Dr. Stein outside the door thumbing through my chart. He opened the door just a bit, stuck his head in and said, "THE AFRICAN QUEEN, I presume."

Emergency Operation

Leonard Tuchyner

(Third place nonfiction, Blue Ridge Writers VWC, 2013)

I am on the edge of worry. She says the pain is getting worse. The ache is an old, intimate acquaintance. She bears it stoically, as is her way. Surely, this ache will pass in the way of its bothersome brothers in times before. (I tell myself.)

She has been testy this evening. No fault of mine, but that of an inconvenient discomfort. It will pass. Such thoughts are comforting.

Time grinds slowly onward. The malady rides along on its back—a poisonous slug digging into quivering flesh. It is a chore to keep its presence in the dark rooms of my mind—a specter one tries not to see.

Twelve midnight. Talk of emergency rooms peeks through the curtains of resistance. Concern blossoms into bilious worry.

One a.m. My wife struggles urgently out of bed, driven by intense bathroom needs. Horrible hacking vomit sounds. They extend into an endless series—a tortured spirit expelling swallowed demons, mortified at what issues from its mouth. Worry explodes into knife-edged fear.

"Oh God, call 911. I need to go to the emergency room," she gasps.

While waiting, I rush to gather things. Heart and mind races. Diane huddles on the couch. Her dog cuddles protectively against her. My dog, Barney, is tense, his movement frenetic, random, confused.

One thirty a.m. Phone rings. A woman's voice, "The rescue squad can't find your house."

"Describe where they are," I say. Miraculously, my voice is calm, my head clear. "Describe their surroundings."

"They're in a cul-de-sac on top of a hill," she answers.

"There are two cul-de-sacs and two hills. One is just above my house. I'm going out to look. My cordless phone may disconnect. I could lose contact with you."

The winter night is cold. Inappropriately beautiful half-moon light enables my half-blind eyes to navigate as far as the end of my driveway.

"Are you still with me, sir?"

A mix of incompatible thankfulness and dread emotions engulf me as I see flashing lights on the hilltop—red lights of Christmas and of devouring fire.

"Tell them to drive down the hill, and I'll wave them in."

At the door, Chloe and Barney make their usual frenzied welcome—tails wagging—the hound barking and howling—the little dog jumping and prancing on hind legs. Chloe cuts it short to return to her mistress's side. The two burley men put the dogs at ease—veterans of canine encounters in human rescues. Chloe does not challenge them as they ask her mistress questions and take her vitals. But when I try to move her from Diane's side, to put her in the basement, she snarls and bares her teeth. I dare not push this to a contest of wills. I know she will cooperate once her mistress is gone. Somehow, she tells me so.

Diane walks to the ambulance without complaint. Thus is her strong, soft manner. Chloe howls mournfully from the basement. Diane is secured to the ambulance gurney. One rescuer plies his saving arts. I am not allowed in the back of the truck to be with her.

A narrow three-foot tunnel separates us. Strewn with impediments, it is three miles long.

I worm and climb my way through and rub her head to let her know I'm there.

"Can you go back in and get my purse?"

I struggle back to the front and search blindly for the door release. After an eternity, my fingers find the lever.

"Why can't they put these things in the same place of every vehicle? If there were a fire, I'd be fried."

At the front door, the unlocking procedure proceeds in a fumbling, bumbling farce. When I get back they are ready to leave.

"Wait a minute. I've got to go back. I don't have hearing aid batteries."

"Is that absolutely necessary? We've got to get going."

"If my batteries go bad, I can't communicate."

He resists saying anything more, and I'm out the door. My hand shakes at the keyhole.

The ambulance is a lumbering elephant climbing the extreme hill, with lights flashing in a silent 2:00 a.m. morning. Inside the huge, high vehicle, we move slowly through a black-and-white dreamscape of midtown lights that stand like mournful, unfeeling observers to a tragedy seen nightly, as they watch us drift by. The sound of the engine whispers in a soft chugging cadence, belying its actual speed—a diesel tugboat making its way through empty city streets.

Against the other-worldliness, the reality of Diane's pain makes my eyes weep. I turn away from the driver and stare out the window.

In the Emergency Room

A gurney is hard and narrow, not a comfort cot at all, made only for transport and utility. It's a foreboding piece of soulless equipment. Its hard, noisy wheels bounce across the pavement toward the emergency entrance. A gurney has no regard for warm, throbbing flesh that harbors my wife's traumatized soul. Ambient light floods the pavement and shows us the way to the cold glass doors—a light that holds hope and dread.

As we enter, my mind is only dimly aware of details—a corridor, innocuous narrow doors on the left. They must be storage-room doors. What are they keeping behind those doors? I wonder. A few people mill around down the hall. Our EMTs open one door and begin to maneuver Diane's gurney into a small emergency room.

A man's groan grinds out from behind a white curtain in a corner of the room. Some kind of station occupies the far center. Someone in hospital garb stands studying a computer screen, her back to us. She offers no greeting or recognition of our presence.

126

Diane is rolled next to a larger mobile bed sitting in a vacant corner. Safety rails are lowered and she scoots herself from one to the other. She seems not to have moved throughout the ambulance journey. This animation of her body stirs a whisper of optimism.

The two-man rescue squad leaves, and with them the gurney, which, in that instant of endless eternity, had become so much a part of our lives.

Now there is a bigger gurney. A woman comes to my wife's bed and starts putting monitors and tubes on and into her. Other workers walk through on nameless tasks. I am in an ant colony or aboard a Borg space cube, witnessing drones going about their somehow-related jobs, desensitized to the human drama that surrounds them.

The bed is pressed close to a wall on its left. Within the narrow space that remains is a spaghetti tangle of tubes and wires. Half hidden within that mass is an uncomfortable-looking small metal chair. A TV screen is mounted high on that wall. Murmuring, meaningless sounds emanate from a speaker on a shelf on Diane's right.

Behind another white curtain, a woman is talking about her leg in pleasant, sociable tones. The man groans—louder this time.

I squeeze and twist my way through the tubes and wires to the unwelcoming chair to sit and wait. As an afterthought, a drone draws our cubicle's white curtain around us. It walls off nothing.

Time and people blur in my tired, abused mind. A nurse checks in. My wife asks for more pain medication. Nurse assures her that *eventually* they will get a prescription from a doctor for stronger stuff. *Eventually* she does. It helps a little. We talk to various people—an intern—a resident—another nurse.

One of them says, "We're giving you some dye that will enable a CT scan to show us what's going on inside. It'll take two hours to infiltrate your system enough to enable the machine to do its job."

It's about 4:00 a.m. We're alone. I'm too keyed up, too tired, and too uncomfortable to sleep in that hard metal chair, hidden in the wire and tube jungle. Behind the other white curtains come the sounds of the suffering man and the jabbering of the loquacious woman describing the state of her injured leg. To whom?

I step outside the room into a corridor and head for a nearby exit, which I've been told is a waiting room with comfortable chairs. A large woman approaches me. She looks at me as though I were a prisoner in an out-of-bounds area. She is a guard—a security guard—and I am in a restricted area.

"Can I help you?"

Her voice belies her interest in helping me. It's accusatory and tells me I should proceed with caution.

"My wife is in that room. It's an emergency. I'm legally blind, so I'm not sure exactly where I am. I was told there was a waiting room where I could rest for a while."

Her whole demeanor changes. Now she really is interested in being helpful.

"You need a pass to be here. Then you can go and come any time."

When I get my pass, the locked emergency room doors open magically whenever I come or go.

I find the waiting room just around the corner from the security doors. Soft, straight-backed chairs are waiting for me. But it is unlawful to move them from their side-by-side regimented rows. There is no way to raise my legs. After ten minutes, I'm back with Diane.

Six a.m. They take her for the CT scan. I try to sleep in the waiting room. No luck. In twenty minutes Diane is back. I listen to the verdict.

"You have a twisted colon. It's being choked off from its blood supply and not allowing any food to pass through. Sometimes we can go in and straighten it out, but it is apt to happen again. We'll have to wait for the surgeon to decide. She'll be here *shortly*."

By this time I am inured to waiting. It has become my way of life. So it seems that *shortly* was a reasonable description.

"An operation is imperative," she informs us. "It has to happen this morning. Even if we could straighten out your colon, it is apt to kink again."

"How long do you expect the procedure to take?" I ask.

"Two to four hours."

"Will you have someone reach me to tell me how it went?"

"Of course. You should hear from us by 2:00 p.m."

I call my son. He is on vacation. His voice is groggy. Ben knows nothing of what has been happening to his mother. I fill him in.

"Is she going to be OK?"

"Yes. There can be complications, but the statistics are all on our side." I listen to my own words, because it helps me to believe in them. My mind knows that what I am saying is true, but the immediate reality is one of uncertainty.

"Do you need a ride home?"

"I have a meeting at the house this morning. I'll call one of our group members to see if she can pick me up. But I'll need a ride back to the hospital. I can't tell you when, exactly. At this moment, I don't know anything exactly."

A big hooked question mark is lodged in my gut, and I wish it would go away.

The Hospital Experience

I wait until I'm fairly confident that Sigrid, my writing group member, has had time to awaken and get the dust out of her eyes. I feel somewhat reluctant to begin asking for special help from friends, but I know it is a necessity. Being legally blind limits independence, whether I like it or not. I wrestle with that obnoxious reality daily.

"Sigrid, this is Leonard."

"What's up?"

"I've been at the hospital with Diane since last night. She's being prepped for emergency surgery."

"Oh, my God. What happened?"

"Diane needs emergency surgery. I think it's going to be fine. I'll fill in the details later."

"How can I help?"

"Well, I can use a ride back home, if you don't mind picking me up at the hospital. I know it's asking a lot, and my son is available if you can't do it"

"Of course I'll get you home. It's on my way to our meeting anyway. Are you sure you still want to have the meeting?"

"Yes. It will get my mind off my worries. But I'm not sure any of the other members are going to make it today. So I'll understand if you back out."

"Don't be silly. I'm getting ready to leave now. I'll be there in an hour. I'll meet you in the main lobby."

"You know I won't be able to see you."

"I'll find you."

In Retrospect

The days that followed were a roller coaster of emotions. They ranged from anxiety, hope, frustration, despair, to gratitude and elation. The details are blurred in some ways and fire-sharp in others.

Today, I am often filled with amazement and gratitude for the help that came to our rescue by neighbors and other friends. This appreciation was felt throughout the ordeal of getting past hospitalization, but the anxiety and depression were often too overwhelming to give thankfulness adequate expression.

I had expectations that my wife would be coming home the day after the operation. I had undergone life-saving and other serious operations before and had always returned home the same day or at least the day after. So I thought it reasonable that she would do the same. Obviously, I'd seriously underestimated the degree of trauma that had been rendered. Still, the nurses I'd spoken to via telephone had not discouraged the optimism. They should have—it might have saved me a little consternation.

"Everything went well," the recovery room nurse informed me. "We're taking her up to her room now. You can call her there in about thirty minutes."

Muscles I didn't even realize were tense, unclamped. After a hot shower, I called her room.

"Hello?" Her voice was sultry-sleepy. Obviously, she was feeling no pain.

"Hi, it's me."

"Leonard?"

"Yeah, that's the one, your husband."

A little giggle, then silence.

"Hello," I said.

"Oh, did I just say something?" she asked.

"You said, 'Hello.'"

"Oh." Silence.

I wade through the conversation with an amused heart.

"I'll call Ben so he'll know he can visit today. I'll be there tomorrow. Maybe you can come home by then."

"I hope so."

"I love you," I say in closing.

"I love y—" Silence.

I knew from that brief conversation that she wasn't coming home that day. But I did expect her return on the morrow.

I called twice more that afternoon and night. She became increasingly alert but was clearly heavily dosed on narcotics. Diane was still in Happy Land. I agreed to bring her Kindle and some other items when I was to arrive the next morning. In my mind, it would give her something to do until she came home that afternoon.

But the next morning my good mood was dashed when I was informed she would not be released that day.

The head nurse said, "We don't want her leaving when her temperature is so high. It's nothing to be concerned about. Give it another day. Most patients don't go home after this kind of surgery so soon."

I thought to myself, If there isn't anything to be concerned about, why can't she come home? Certainly a high temperature can be dealt with at home where there is less chance of infection. I was beginning to get the feeling that we were not being told everything. Wouldn't the high temperature mean there was already an infection?

However, Diane was still in a good mood. We went for a short walk a few doors down the corridor. She needed a walker to steady herself, and the IV bags had to go along with us.

By the third day, the story was the same. The temperature was still the problem. Diane's mood was changing, and she was expressing strong desires to leave the hospital. She was particularly distressed about not having a window to look out. She also had a new roommate about whom she felt considerably uncomfortable.

I almost felt myself getting into an argument with the nurse regarding the folly of keeping her there.

The fourth day things seemed to be turning around, finally. The IV tubes were gone. The temperature was down, and the doctors told her she could come home the next day.

But later in the afternoon Diane called me at home.

"Hello?" I answered.

"It's me. I want to come home."

"You're coming home tomorrow. Remember? If they don't let you go, just walk out. You're not a prisoner. They can't keep you there. I'll tell Ben to come pick you up, no matter what."

Her voice got very soft.

"I can hardly hear you."

"I can't talk louder. They're listening."

"Who's listening?"

"I can't tell you now. My roommate—"

"What about your roommate?"

"I can't tell you." Her voice sounded scared.

"I don't even know where I am. I'm too far away from the window."

"You're at the hospital."

"Are you sure?"

"Of course I'm sure. What's happened?"

"I can't talk."

I imagined her looking suspiciously around for an eves dropper.

"Have you told the nurses how you feel?"

"I can't. They're part of the problem."

"Let me talk to one of them."

"No! You'll make it worse."

"Look, you'll be out of the hospital tomorrow, and everything will be fine. That place is driving you crazy."

"I need to come home."

"I'll see you here tomorrow. I can't wait."

Suddenly, I was back in anxiety and depression. Diane was having paranoid delusions, something that was entirely unique for her. I was convinced staying in the hospital was only going to make it worse, and I was having my own nutty thoughts. Both of our sanities depended on her leaving.

I called early the fifth day.

"Hi, it's me. Bring me up to date."

"It's better. They moved me into a new room next to a window. I know I'm still in the hospital now. I thought I'd been abducted to someplace out of Charlottesville. I'm away from that awful roommate."

"That's good. Have the doctors made their rounds yet?"

"They don't want me to leave."

"Why?"

"They want me here another day. They'll look in on me this evening to decide about tomorrow. But I don't want to stay another minute. I'm going home today."

"I think that's a great idea. There's no reason they can't treat you as an outpatient. I'll call Ben to help you pack. Call me when you're ready to leave. They won't like it, but there's nothing they can do about it. You're not a prisoner."

The phone rang again at 11:00 a.m.

"They won't let me go. I was walking down the hall with Ben when the resident surgeon stopped me and said if I left, AMA, the insurance company, would not pay for anything."

"That's . . . that's criminal! I'm going to be at the next meeting. I'll get there any way I can."

"Good!"

I got there just in time. I felt like a bomb about to explode. But I was glad to see my wife back to her old self.

When the surgeon arrived, I lost no time in confronting him.

133

"What's going on? There are things I don't understand. What are you keeping from us? Diane would have been much better off at home."

"I agree," the resident said, disarming me in the process. His voice and personality were hard not to like. "I am a champion of people going home as soon as possible. Hospitals are not the best places for healing."

"Then why . . . ?"

"When we first talked to your wife, she was a different person than she was yesterday. Suddenly, her thinking and emotions seemed way out of kilter. We thought she was reacting to the medication, but we couldn't be sure. Something could have been going wrong in the healing process. Now I see she is back to normal since we changed her meds. I want her to leave first thing tomorrow morning."

"You can't know how happy that makes me. But I've got to tell you, you guys did a lousy job in the communication department. Everything you've just told us is new material. I could have helped Diane to feel better if I'd known the score. I believed the staff was blowing smoke you know where. I was at a point where I didn't trust anything they were telling us."

"We don't always do the best job of communicating. I'm sorry about that."

"Can you keep me in the loop from here on out?"

"Definitely."

We smiled at each other, and I felt the weight of the world lifting off my shoulders. I thought, "What a nice guy."

"Well, we have other patients to see. If you'll excuse us . . ."

"Thanks for listening, Doctor."

Next morning, Ben brought his mother home.

Why Certainty in Science Is Unscientific (Or, Turning Richard Dawkins on His Head)

Cornelia Clay Fulghum

Celebrity biologist and avowed atheist Richard Dawkins is in the habit of making headlines by attacking those whose worldview is influenced not just by science but by religion and philosophy as well. He is a science apologist *nonpareil*, averring that science offers us everything we need to nurture our lives. I have caught him out, however, in a violation of his principles, as he just can't manufacture any delight in the implications of the second law of thermodynamics. Indeed, this foundational law of physics seems to have the power to depress science's most indefatigable cheerleader.

Writing in 1996, in the online magazine *The Humanist*, Dawkins declares: "(W)e know from the second law of thermodynamics (which predicts that isolated systems will eventually wind down) that all complexity, all life, all laughter, all sorrow is hell-bent on leveling itself out into cold nothingness in the end. They—and we—can never be more than temporary, local, buckings of the great universal slide into the abyss of uniformity."

This statement, profoundly negative in tone, demonstrates that, at the very least, his is a complicated response to impermanence on a universal scale. It is a rare (but telling) instance in which he appears disappointed in reality as it is revealed by science.

He's right, of course, that no one has yet shown the second law can be violated; fortunes are not being made on the stock market from investments in perpetual motion machines. The heat death of the universe (meaning, ironically, the cessation of movement in cold, empty space), predicted by the second law, may indeed transpire.

But to speak decisively, authoritatively, of an apocalyptic event that may—or may not—occur billions of years in the future seems an inappropriate scientific extrapolation.

Cyclic Uncertainties

Yes, the second law does point to a universal winding down. But consider this: Our familiar universe just might come into and out of existence over and over again.

Cyclic theories such as those proposed by Paul Steinhardt and Neil Turok as well as by Lauris Baum and Paul Frampton circumvent conversion of everything into "cold nothingness in the end." Eric Chaisson's work, based on Nobelist Ilya Prigogine's far-from-equilibrium thermodynamics, has also brought into question the heat death scenario.

As for cosmology, we are in the middle of a fascinating wrangle. Various theories depict our possible fate. Uncertainty rules, and this is as it should be.

Even Dawkins has admitted to the mysteriousness of the universe, especially as it is revealed by quantum mechanics. He's just forgotten that admission here.

He knows the science, of course. But he's not consoled. Indeed, he seems distressed that our human experience has no obvious value or meaning. Like many other atheists who deny that God has reserved a unique place in the scheme of things for man, he's still a bit upset that it's not the case.

Dawkins, Dissatisfied with Science?

There's no getting around it. For a brief moment, the great science apologist, Richard Dawkins, was at odds with science. His words even hint that he would be happier with a kinder, gentler universe, one disposed toward the human race. (It's hard not to think of conventional religious views, in this context.)

He's missing the mark, of course. We should not feel estranged from our world because of physical laws, much less because of our theories about catastrophes those laws might bring to pass. This is just drawing out bitterness from abstraction.

Let us mourn, lament, and rejoice. Let us feel all the

pleasure and pain it is our lot to feel, holding dear our extraordinary lives and our extraordinary world, at once so beautiful and so terrible. But let us refrain from making into something personal the notion of inescapable cosmological disaster.

We just don't know enough to take such speculation seriously. There are important, pertinent matters we don't have a clue about. For example, the provenance of our physical laws—indeed their very nature—is unknown. We can't ascertain if they are human impositions onto the majestic chaos of reality or if they possess transcendent reality, as the mathematics suggests. (We have the same predicament with mathematics itself.)

If we did, in fact, "discover" the so-called laws of nature, and they have an objective and primordial existence exactly as we have formulated them, who's to say even then that we have arrived at the final, ultimate, algorithms?

And if they are primordial, *what* caused them to come into being in the first place? It's impossible to explain how everything got started without positing a prior term. Infinite regress is unavoidable. Dawkins should remember how he himself rebuffed the existence of God as a final term by asking what brought God into existence.

No Methodological Errors, Please

We are small creatures in the prodigious scheme of things. The known universe consists of a hundred billion galaxies and a hundred billion stars in each of them. From our vantage point on Earth, we work day and night to unravel the unknowns of this ever-expanding cosmos and properly rejoice at our findings when they appear confirmed.

Over three hundred years of modern science have gone into our current understanding of the nature of things. It's great!

Let's just not forget the big picture, as we spin around our radiant star. We can—and must—try to figure out all the minutiae of existence. But we need always to keep in mind that we are doing so from a point of view limited in space and time and limited by the nature of our own human brains.

Cosmologist Stephen Hawking, probably the most well-known scientific figure of our time, would agree. In his 2010 book, *The Grand Design*, he maintains that there is no theory-independent reality; we are preprogrammed to see what we see by the nature of our expectations. We undeniably filter everything through the categories of our own minds. We cannot apprehend reality except through the lens of our human consciousness. Our data are massaged from the outset by the human factor.

We would do well to admit: All-that-is is more than our minds can comprehend. A modicum of humility is in order, here on this "pale blue dot" of Earth.

And isn't humility the most scientifically respectful position to stake out, choosing to make as few assumptions as possible, in light of the hypothesized multiverse, with its infinity of universes besides our own?

Here's my point: Not to acknowledge the mystery that underlies our experience—and that underlies, as well, our great human enterprise of science—is a serious methodological error.

Nobody, not even Richard Dawkins, should waste one moment of life bemoaning the personal implications of scientific theorizing.

Mother of the Bride

Phyllis R. Koch-Sheras

"At the wedding tomorrow, when I am asked if I am willing to give our daughter away, I will say 'no.' (You can hear a gasp among the rehearsal dinner guests.) That is because Phyllis and I feel like we are not giving her up. We are sharing her with her beloved and a whole new family."

Peter, always the consummate speaker, has just finished giving a witty and moving toast at a dinner the night before the marriage of our daughter, Samantha, to her wonderful fiancé, Don. Now it's my turn to address the small, but lively, group in the private room of a trendy Italian restaurant in Santa Barbara.

"Summertime and the livin' is easy . . . Oh, your Daddy's rich and your Momma's good lookin' . . . So hush, little baby, don't you cry." Those lines from "Summertime" seem like the best way to start my toast at this lovely rehearsal dinner. They were the words to the "lullaby" I sang to you, Samantha, every night—until you fell asleep. Then you stopped asking for it—too old for it, I guess—until now that you and Don are getting married, and you asked me to sing it at the wedding reception tomorrow. My baby—grown up? I guess so! I still remember you calling us and crying for us to come pick you up from overnight camp because you were homesick. Now here you are all the way out in California—and not crying at all.

"A few weeks ago, Don, you asked us to send you some 'embarrassing' photos of Samantha for a slide show you were putting together for the wedding—not just the 'cute' pictures that she had picked out. 'Nobody's that perfect,' you said. 'It's like she never made a bad fashion decision. Hook me up with some dirt here, please,' you requested. I couldn't really come up with anything embarrassing—not even in my mind's eye. Well, maybe 'yes' during a few of those challenging adolescent years. She was hell on wheels then, as a matter of fact. Like the time she threw her club when she missed a putt at the miniature golf course. Not necessarily something for a Kodak moment, however.

"I did find pictures of Samantha in a pink tutu smiling from ear to ear . . . photos of her and her friends posing on the beach, tilting her head back and looking over her shoulder at the camera like a model (her favorite camera angle!) . . . dancing with her father at her Bat Mitzvah—him looking at her lovingly as she peeks coyly at me taking the picture . . . dressed in her soccer uniform, sticking out her tongue at the camera . . . sitting at the World Cup Soccer tournament with a satisfied, dreamy look on her face—'seventh heaven,' I guess, for a dedicated soccer player . . . sitting on the front steps of our house just before her high school graduation, hugging our dog, Hollie—both of them posing as if for a formal photograph.

"I started crying weeks before she left for college, anticipating her moving half way across the country. I still remember that summer night when Peter was out of town, and I was driving to a retreat out in the country by myself:

"It's raining, and I miss my turn. I make a U-turn and suddenly I feel a car smashing full speed right into my driver's side. My car is totaled, but I am not hurt. I start hyperventilating. Someone calls the police. I call Samantha and ask her to pick me up. She tells me she'll come right over. 'Stay calm, Mom, you're all right,' she says sweetly. 'What will I do without you?' I cry. 'You'll be fine, Mom.' She drives me home (such a good driver, just like her dad). Just before we get out of the car, she kisses my cheek. 'I love you, Mom,' she says.

"At that moment, I knew you had grown up, Samantha. I did my best to cherish every minute we had together during the next couple of months before you left for college. . . . I'm sorry. I'm getting emotional here. Who's having trouble separating now? . . . Not you, Samantha, all grown up—and creating your own family.

"'One of these mornin's you're going' to rise up singing. And you'll spread your wings, and you'll take to the sky. Until that morning, there is nothing can harm you—with Mammy and Daddy standin' by.'

"I'm always here with you, Samantha—and now for your couple, too--standing by. And I know you're always with me. Go now together and take to the sky! I love you, too."

A few days later, after the wedding, sitting next to Peter as he sleeps on our red-eye flight back from California, sipping a glass of wine, thoughts are racing through my mind:

It's a lot easier said than done—this giving away of your only daughter to an almost perfect stranger! Not like I really got to "give her away." There's no part for the mother who gave *birth* to this bride in the whole darn wedding ceremony. And that's pretty hard to take, especially for a diva like me! I never really noticed it before—not until I had the unheralded role of "mother of the bride." Plus, come to think of it, what's this about "giving away" the bride anyway? What is she? A piece of property or something?!

I loved that Samantha and Don agreed to include the breaking of the glass at the end of the wedding ceremony—even though Don was afraid of getting glass in his sandal-clad foot. (I guess you can't expect someone who is not Jewish to understand that kind of thing.) I felt more than just the glass break as Don stepped on it. I shouldn't be so dramatic, I guess but it was like cutting the umbilical cord all over again. You're off on your honeymoon now, and I'm wondering if we'll still talk on the phone every other day. Now that you're a married woman, will you still want to come "home" and visit? Living on opposite ends of the country doesn't make it any easier.

I can't really sleep on these flights. So many unanswered questions I didn't think to ask: How did you like my singing of "Summertime" at the wedding? Why didn't I take any pictures of you with Don in your wedding dress? When is it OK to call you next?

* * * *

I'm exhausted, and all I want to do is go home and get into bed. And what do you know? I open the door to Peter's Volvo station wagon as we leave the airport in cold, rainy Virginia and smash the edge of the door right into my face. I manage to split my lip right open. Blood is spurting now, but it's nothing compared to the internal blow I'm feeling. What is it? Sadness, anger, loss, grief? I'm so happy for Samantha and Don, but I can't stop crying!

Maybe I needed that smack in the face. "It's an appropriate time to bleed," a friend told me yesterday after I told her what happened. Wake up to reality. Let her go. Don't be so attached. "Accept impermanence," my Tibetan Buddhist teacher would say. Will I ever learn?

I'm all stitched up now, and the wound is healing. My internal wounds—my sense of loss and fear of change—are slowly healing, too. I'm not giving you up, Samantha. Like Peter said in his toast, we're sharing you with your husband and your new family. Your phone call as you drove to the airport on the way to your honeymoon was so nice. Maybe you won't forget about your dear old mom after all—even if you do have a different last name now that I still have trouble pronouncing. It's just you spreading "your wings as you take to the sky."

The Day Anastasia Ticked Off Rasputin's Daughter

Gary D. Kessler

We all have mysteries of life events that make us stop occasionally and wonder "What about that?" Like what happened to Amelia Earhart? Where is Jimmy Hoffa wearing his cement shoes? Did Marilyn Monroe really commit suicide? Did Anastasia really survive the massacre of the Russian imperial family? While time and DNA have answered the last question (the answer being "no," by the way), it's a question that's had a wild and fascinating ride and, for some reason, has left me scratching my head on just what Anna Anderson/Anastasia said to Rasputin's daughter on that day in November 1968 in Charlottesville, Virginia, that ticked Maria off. (What? That's not on your list of burning questions? Do tell.) I've heard that it was that "Russian grand duchesses do not 'dine out.'" I've always rather hoped that *is* what she said—especially since Maria's famous father's big mistake was just that, dining out.

The Anastasia fable—that the youngest daughter of Tsar Nicholas II (along, perhaps, with the thirteen-year-old tsarevitch, Alexei) survived the slaughter of the Russian imperial family in a mine shaft in Ekaterinburg in 1918 at the hands of Russian revolutionaries—is one that flourished for a good half century and took on some fascinating under- and overtones. If you mention "The Recognition Scene" to almost anyone in the theater, for instance, they will instantly hone in on the second act of the Guy Bolton Broadway play *Anastasia*, which has been used repeatedly in auditions and one-act competitions. In its 1956 movie form, it won Ingrid Bergman an Academy Award, as the pretender Anastasia, set off against the imposing character of the Dowager Empress Marie Feodorovna, played by the "First Lady of the American Theater," Helen Hayes.

The play cleverly hedges on whether the dowager empress recognizes the pretender as her granddaughter, Anastasia, but, doing what Hollywood so often does, weaves the scene to leave the impression that she very much wants to believe the young woman is Anastasia. In real life, Marie Feodorovna denounced the pretender Anna Anderson from the very beginning through to her last royal breath.

There have been several pretenders to having been a surviving Anastasia, but none were as resilient and interesting—and, possibly, as bizarre—as the woman who eventually became known as Anna Anderson. The main focus of the Russian succession conundrum crossed the Atlantic when Anderson last arrived on the shores of the United States in 1968, brought to America—and Charlottesville, Virginia—by Gleb Botkin, the son of Tsar Nicholas' family doctor, Eugene Botkin, who was murdered with the imperial family. Thanks to the march of science and time, Anna Anderson has been revealed to have been a sometimes/sometimes not insane former Polish factory worker, Franziska Schanzkowska.

Franziska first turned up in connection with the Anastasia story in 1920 with amnesia and, legend says, speaking Russian and muttering information that only the tsar's family would know, after being fished out the river in Berlin, Germany, in the throes of a botched suicide attempt. First hinted to be a different imperial sister, Tatiana, and only later as Anastasia, Anna spent the next eight years traveling around Europe, being rejected as Anastasia by nearly everyone who would have reason to know Anastasia, while at the same time being supported and housed by various expatriate members of the Russian imperial family when she wasn't being locked up in an asylum.

There were times when it looked like everyone around Anna also was a bit mad.

The reason for this contradictory behavior by the expatriate Russian royals became apparent in 1928 when the ten-year waiting period of an unproved death of Tsar Nicholas was over for dispersing the tsar's supposed banked wealth outside of Russia to the nearest of established kin. You couldn't get any nearer than the immediate family in satisfying a bank when everyone else was disputing who was nearer beyond that. So from 1928 on for forty years, Anastasia became even more someone to hedge on, to keep close, and also to debunk in public—until it became convenient to suddenly recognize her as legitimate. As it turns out, all of this maneuvering was on speculation for an foreign fortune that was never located beyond a small deposit in Germany. Still, into the sixties most of the Romanovs stuck with declaring Anna a fraud, while continuing to support her financially and shunt her around from castle to castle in Europe, with a brief three-year stay in the States. Her list of supporters grew too. A faction led by the Botkins—Eugene Botkin's daughter, Tatiana, and son, Gleb—mounted legal suits to have Anna declared to be Anastasia.

Suits and welcomes finally worn out, Gleb Botkin brought Anna to the States on a six-month visitor's visa in 1968, and University of Virginia history professor, John (Jack) Manahan, more than a little eccentric himself, married Anna before the visa expired so she wouldn't be deported. This was her second sojourn in the States; she was in New York between 1928 and 1930, being shuffled between the estates of supporters and, again, insane asylums. This could be called her "musical" period. She went by the name Anna/Anastasia Tschaikovsky while living at an Oyster Bay estate and was moved to a Hempstead, New York, hotel for a period by the composer and pianist Sergei Rachmaninoff before, once again, being relegated to an asylum.

Anna was deported as insane to Germany, where she was immediately declared sane but permitted to live in an asylum because she had no place else to go. Prince Frederick of Saxe-Altenburg picked her up next and settled her in a cottage on the edge of the Black Forest in Germany, where she lived and functioned as a local shrine to those curious about the Romanovs, real or otherwise, along with an Irish wolfhound and sixty cats, until she was found unconscious on her cottage floor one day and hospitalized. Finding, in horror, that her menagerie had been euthanized while she was in the hospital, Anna accepted a long-extended invitation by Gleb Botkin to join him in Virginia.

Gleb Botkin died in Charlottesville in 1969, which, along with the absence of an imperial fortune to be found in European banks, brought an effective end to the Anastasia suits. Anna and her new husband, Jack Manahan, lived quietly and a bit strangely in Charlottesville until she died in 1984 and he in 1990—with a brief sort of Bonnie and Clyde escapade in 1983, when Jack kidnapped her from a Charlottesville hospital and drove her all over Virginia for three days, feeding her from convenience stores.

Although Manahan did like to refer to himself as the tsar's son-in-law from time to time, he was enough of a colorful local figure in his own right—and rich enough to get away with his eccentricities—for people in the community to just smile at the couple's occasional shenanigans. When I asked him once why he'd married her—it obviously was a marriage of convenience—he told me that whether or not Anna really was Anastasia was beside the point—that she had been used and abused by so many for so long that he thought she deserved to live out her life in peace with someone taking care of her. The residents of Charlottesville pretty much left the couple alone to serve that end and, being used to having celebrities in their midst, protected the couple's privacy.

Mercifully for Anna, she wasn't scientifically debunked through DNA testing (which stalwarts are still disputing—not that the hair used from a hairbrush didn't trace back to Franziska Schanzkowska, but, rather, that the tested hair wasn't Anna's) for a decade after she died. In the eighty years following her splash in the river in Berlin, Anna Anderson was nearly the sole inspiration of countless books, plays, movies, and even a ballet based on the life of the resurrected Anastasia. The last of these seems to have been a 1997 animated children's film favorably treating her claim.

Maria Rasputin, born Matryona, but called "Maria" by her parents, had led a much different, but just as colorful life, up to the point that she met Anna Anderson for the first time. Maria was the daughter of one of history's other enduring fascinating historical Russian figures, the "mad monk" Grigori Rasputin, a Russian mystic who captured the fancy and full compliance of the Empress Alexandra, both because of her own mystic tendencies and because she believed Rasputin could save and protect the tsarevitch, a hemophiliac. Rasputin was a dark, foreboding character, who obtained and maintained so much control over the imperial family that other Russian nobles, coveting that influence for themselves, invited him to a dinner party outside the imperial palace in 1916 and, they claimed, dispatched him by poisoning, stabbing, and drowning. The various means used, the length of time they acknowledged it took for the monk to die, and that only his boots were ever found to verify the deed, have only added to his own "What about that?" legend.

A year later, Maria's father's followers convinced her to marry the hypnotist Boris Soloviev, Grigori Rasputin's successor among the mystics, who hypnotized funds out of several of the Romanovs in schemes to smuggle them out of the country during the throes of revolution. He did manage to get Maria and himself out to Romania, though, where he worked in sideshows in Bucharest and she as a cabaret dancer. The couple went on to Paris, where Boris worked in an automobile factory and died of tuberculoses in 1926. They weren't a close couple. Maria said in her memoir that she never liked him and that he didn't touch her, preferring his many mistresses over her. "Naturally," Maria became a circus performer in Ringling Brothers' European circus and moved up to be a lion tamer. She came to the States in the 1930s; got bitten by one of her lions in Peru, Indiana; ditched the circus in Miami; and went on to yet another fascinating career, that of being a riveter in a defense factory.

1965 found Maria in Hollywood, under the wing of Hearst Publications film and theater columnist Patte Barhan, playing on having inherited her father's gift for the supernatural. It very well may have been Barhan who suggested that Maria's act would quadruple its appeal in Hollywood by becoming a duo with the "surviving" Grand Duchess Anastasia.

Knowing that Anastasia/Anna Anderson had arrived back in the States—in Charlottesville, Virginia—under Gleb Botkin's sponsorship in early 1968, Patte Barhan and Maria Rasputin arranged a meeting with Anna through Botkin. They traveled to Charlottesville from Los Angeles for the first of two meetings between the Russian historical figures on Tuesday, August 13, 1968. When they met, Maria claimed the two had been close friends as young children and even that Maria had seen the imperial family leave St. Petersburg for their last exile in Ekaterinburg. Anna apparently didn't remember any of that— obviously because she wasn't really Anastasia, but Anna always had been careful and adroit about who Anastasia remembered knowing and who she didn't.

Both sides had something to gain from the meeting, even beyond the minor publicity the face to face was given in the media. Barhan and Rasputin were looking to put together a psychic act to play Hollywood and maybe even Las Vegas. And, for Botkin and Anderson, Maria was prepared to declare to the world—and did, in fact, do so at this meeting—that Anna Anderson was the true Anastasia. The meeting went swimmingly; you can even buy a coffee mug through the Internet with a photo inlay of the two women smiling and conversing during this meeting, if you like. Whatever was agreed to, though, Anna didn't go to Hollywood.

There was a second, shorter meeting, in November 1968, with, again, Maria Rasputin and Patte Barhan traveling to Charlottesville with more detailed plans for a "sister" Russian diva psychics' act in California. Maria apparently said they would do the party circuit together in Hollywood and dine out with the stars. It was at this point that Anna has been reported to have said, "Russian grand duchesses do not 'dine out.'" The next day, at an airport in Washington, D.C., Maria Rasputin gave a press conference declaring that Anna Anderson was not Anastasia, but just another imposter. Anna married Jack Manahan, twenty years her junior, in Charlottesville on December 23, 1968. Maria Rasputin died in obscurity in 1979.

Thus ends, thanks mostly to DNA science, and fills out, in one of the more bizarre and fascinating ways, one of those "What about that?" mysteries of life events—well, one of my burning questions, if not yours. It appears that the truth of some "What about that?" events are more fantastic than fiction. And it leaves us to inch our way toward the unraveling of maybe—but maybe not—equally interesting conundrums about Marilyn's suicide, the concretization of Jimmy, and/or Amelia's final landing.

Maybe you'll run across one of these people some day when you are dining out.

.

ON WRITING AND PUBLISHING

Don't Iron Your Clothes While They're on Your Body No Matter How Late You Are

Deborah M. Prum

One night years ago I'm supposed to meet my husband and his colleagues downtown at a fancy restaurant at 6:15. It's 6:00. I'm not dressed. My three little kids have not been fed. The babysitter is about to walk in the door.

I'm stirring a pot of Kraft Mac and Cheese with one hand. And I'm running so late that, with the other hand, I'm ironing my black wool pants while I'm wearing them. Worse yet, I'm using a steam iron, which is scalding my legs. But I'm desperate to be on time, so I keep pressing ahead.

The phone rings. I try to answer the call on my cordless phone. No luck. Dead battery. So I head across the room to the wall phone in the kitchen, the one with the very short cord that I had been meaning to replace.

A mellifluous voice comes on the line. She says, "I'm calling from *The Ladies' Home Journal.* May I speak with Deborah Prum?"

Oh no, I don't have time to deal with a subscription spiel. But I had just moved to the South. People here accuse us Northerners of being rude. So, I want to prove them wrong by shedding my Yankee ways. So I say, "This is she, but I have to tell you I currently receive more magazines than I can—"

"I want to talk with you about an idea."

With my short phone cord, I can barely reach the stove, and the orange, goopy mixture of macaroni and cheese begins to burn. "This really isn't a very good time. Could you call back next week?" Or never.

The woman seems taken aback. "Well, I don't think so. We have space for your article in our next issue and the deadline is in a week. I don't think we have the time to discuss it later."

My article? My heart fills with conflicting emotions— elation because I realize she's an editor—someone is finally responding positively to one of my query letters—and panic because I have no idea *which* query letter.

As a beginning freelancer, my recordkeeping is haphazard at best. I don't quite believe my words will ever see the light of day and my approach reflects that zero confidence. Two or three times a week, I'd send off queries to various magazines. As fast as ideas reached my brain, I'd get them down on paper and into the mailbox. Then I'd throw copies of the query letters into a cardboard box I kept in the children's playroom.

While I try to figure out exactly which letter we were talking about, my three hungry sons gather in the kitchen waiting impatiently for their rations to be distributed. I gesture wildly, pantomiming writing on paper with a pen.

My oldest son, Nathaniel, stares at me with feigned concern. Then the prepubescent smart aleck turns to his ten-year-old brother, Eric, and says, "Gosh, it seems as if Mom has developed a tremor."

In the meantime, the editor continues talking. "We like your medical crisis idea."

Medical crisis idea? Now which one would that be: "Lice, the Gift That Keeps on Giving?" or "Cat Dander, the Unseen Foe?" or "Training Your Son to Lower the Lid?"

Desperate for a clue, I try to elicit a hint from her. "Yes, medical crisis. Well, in which direction would you like me to take the concept?"

"We want 1,500 words on how to walk with a friend through a medical crisis. Be sure to give practical pointers and get at least two expert quotes."

By this time, three-year-old Ian recognizes my desperate pleas for a writing implement and gives me a broken orange crayon and half of a paper napkin. I nod at him in thanks and begin scribbling.

As I take notes, Eric spoons supper into a plastic bowl. Then he gives it to Ian, who promptly drops the bowl on the floor and howls.

Silence on the phone. Then, "Am I calling you at your office? Is that a child crying?"

"Yes." I change the subject. "When is the article due?"

Eric gives his little brother a spoon. And Ian, ever the pragmatist, begins eating off of the floor. Unfortunately, my floor has never been one you could eat off of, unless you planned on living a very short life.

The editor sounds curt now, all business. "In a week. We had another article for that spot, but the writer is sick. So we need something else quickly. Do you think you can do it?"

"Sure." I drop my half-napkin down to Ian so he can wipe his face. "No problem."

During the next few days, I can barely contain my excitement. After receiving stacks of rejection letters, I was finally going to have my byline appear in a national magazine. I threw my heart and soul into the project, working late at night after the kids went to bed and early in the morning, before they got up.

That week we entered cruise-control mode for meal preparation. Each morning, the boys woke up to a jug of milk and cereal on the breakfast table. Instead taking the time to make sandwiches, I gave them money to buy lunch at school. For five days straight, supper consisted of greasy brown objects cooked in our microwave: fish sticks, chicken body parts, tiny tacos, and reconstituted potato lumps.

Google did not exist. So, with Ian in tow, I headed for the local library to skim actual books on my topic. Unfortunately, Ian was in the process of being potty trained, so I spent as much time frantically rushing to the bathroom with him as I did in the stacks.

The first draft of the article contained 3,000 words. I pared it down to the required 1,500, agonizing over each word I cut. The final piece included meticulously researched information, comments from both a clinical social worker and a psychiatrist, and a quote from a parent with a chronically ill child. My sidebar listed several tips for handling the situation.

After receiving the article, the editor called to compliment me on the content and quality of the piece. "It's ready to go," she said. "No revisions necessary."

For weeks, I was riding high—*Atlantic Monthly, The New Yorker*, watch out!

Well, two months later as I was arguing with my boys about a candy purchase at the checkout counter of Giant, I noticed a copy of the magazine on the rack. My article title,

"Helping a Friend Through a Medical Crisis" was listed right there on the cover. I pulled the magazine off of the stand and yelled, "Holy cow! I'm real!"

We forgot the candy dispute, and I ripped through the issue trying to find my article. There it was, at the end of the magazine, with my byline plainly in view.

The editor, however, had cut the text to a scant 300 words. She had left my name intact, but not much else. The piece contained a quote from one of my sources and a photo of two women gazing at each other. Maybe one was looking helpful. I'm not sure.

Yes, I felt disappointed. Fortunately, my paycheck arrived in the mailbox the same day. I was so thrilled to be published, I hadn't asked about reimbursement. As it turned out, they paid me five times what I'd ever gotten writing for local publications. Although I mourned that the meat had been ripped from the bones of the article, the fat paycheck helped assuage my grief.

So, what did I do with my windfall? Well, I spent some of the check on very long cord for the kitchen telephone, some on buying a filing cabinet, and the rest on buying a nice pair of black no-iron, wrinkle-free pants.

Ten Ideas How to Get Published

1. Have something to say and make sure you know how to say it well. Have a vision for your work, a reason for why you write.

2. Respect your ideas, your creativity. Treat your ideas with respect by recording them and following through on them.

3. Read broadly. Look for publications you want to approach. Get to know them well. Once you have done that, you will be able to craft an intelligent query letter. Your idea should be novel, but it also should fit into the kind of material they normally publish.

4. Surround yourself with an affirming community of readers/writers who can give honest feedback re: your work and encouragement when you need it. To be safe, you should always have someone check your work before sending it out.

5. Watch for and capitalize on unexpected opportunities. Read trade journals, listen to the radio, watch TV, read newspapers, looking for possibilities. Follow through.

6. Be organized. Keep a file for each article, essay, idea, book, etc. List where you've sent a piece and the response (with dates).

7. Act like a professional. No whining or asking for special favors. Deliver what you promise. Try to establish an ongoing professional relationship with specific editors. Do an excellent job on your first assignment from them. Communicate only when you must. Do not pester an editor, especially if you know that s/he is in the middle of production. Figure out how an editor wants to be approached—e-mail, mail, or phone—and stick to those rules. Get your work in on time and in the format specified. No excuses. If you run into trouble, communicate that quickly, so the editor has time to think of alternatives

8. Make contacts at conferences, lunches, lectures, readings. Accept reading opportunities/panel discussion offers. Support your fellow writers by showing up at their events. Check the back pages of writing magazines and journals to discover new markets. Check online listings and discussion boards.

9. If you think an article, book, essay has merit—be persistent. Keep sending it out. Times change. Editors change.

10. Follow the rules—word count, deadlines, margins, etc. Break the rules. Sometimes it's worth it to follow your intuition and color outside the lines.

Feedback: Where Do You Draw the Line?

Jody Hobbs Hesler

Recently I asked a friend to read the rewrite of a novel chapter I'd revised in response to his original feedback about it. He said he'd be happy to, "But I do have a question for you. Where do you draw the line on other people having input on your art?" A visual artist rather than a writer, he expressed his own skepticism about "people altering the product of my intuition," and so I decided to write an essay about the value of feedback.

At a party a couple years ago, a guest asked me what I got out of other people's comments on my work—I was in a writing group with the host of the party at that time. I said, "It helps me to read my own work more effectively." That was the best answer he said he'd ever gotten to that question. I believe it's the best reason to receive feedback: to help us to become better readers of our own work.

To use feedback this way, we must appoint ourselves masters of our story's vision and then we must trust ourselves to discern what input actually advances our work. Faced with the range of feedback that inevitably comes from any group, how do we develop judgment to do this? How do we avoid turning our rewrite into Frankenstein-ian monster mashes / having people alter the products of our intuition?

We look for feedback that supports our vision—that resonates with us. Some years ago, my chiropractor explained how people diagnosed broken bones before you could get X-rays. You take a tuning fork, give it a whack, and, while it's still vibrating, touch the base of the tuning fork on the bone near the area of the suspected break. Guess what happens? The vibrations of the fork resonate along the bone, and if there's a break, it jiggles and hurts like crap. Feedback should work this same way.

Feedback that's truly interested in the aims our work sets out to achieve—beware the reader who wants all our work to look like his or like whatever's in the latest *New Yorker*—should resonate with us. When there's a break somewhere in the story, good feedback makes it jiggle and hurt. Our writerly faces crimp with discomfort. "Ah, yes. Right there," we think.

One sign of bad feedback is too much specificity: "Your character should say [this] instead of [that]," or, "At the end, your character needs to go back and do [whatever thing] over again." This kind of feedback takes the writer out of that judgment seat and may rush the work to conclusions that have nothing to do with our original vision.

Instead, the best feedback says, "In this scene, when the character does or says [this thing], I stop believing in him," or, "At this moment, I can't picture where we are anymore," or, "In [this scene], you had me the whole time. But when we switched to [this scene], I lost that connection."

In other words, good feedback gives flags that chart our reader's course through their experience of our work. It resonates and shows us exactly where the break is. The challenge after good feedback is figuring out how to solve the problems in those broken places, not how to fit all the reader's ideas into our story.

Back to my artist friend's original feedback. He had responded to a moment when a little girl broke her arm. His concerns about how she and the other characters reacted to the injury resonated with me because they made me realize I hadn't visualized the scene as intensely as I thought I had. I had left things out.

So I pictured the scene over again, deliberately and minutely. I contacted a friend whose daughter broke her arm in a similar way to what I was trying to describe. My friend and her daughter wrote detailed accounts of the break and its aftermath that helped clarify a lot of things for me. I incorporated their input into my rewrite and then sent the chapter along to a family doctor friend to get his medical opinion about my description of the injury and of the characters' reactions. After all that, I sent my chapter back to my artist friend for a second opinion on whether I had solved the problems he had seen.

This is how good feedback works—and how involved a rewrote should be. We get feedback that resonates. We zero in on the broken places, reimagine them in every detail, then layer the rewritten moments back into the story, often rewriting most of the story (or chapter) in that process.

It's a lot of work. That's why it's important to know what we want from feedback and how to use it. And it's important to feel confident enough to identify and dismiss feedback that misses the mark.

Good feedback feels exciting—even when it points out the reappearance of recurring writing bugaboos we're working madly to eradicate, making us think, "Oh, crap. Did I do that again?" Even then, good feedback helps us feel like we're on our way to something better.

What Counts

Jody Hobbs Hesler

We've all had, or read about and admired, mentors who wake up at 4:00 a.m. and work for three hours before anyone else in the house is awake, or who staunchly believe in producing at least one page a day—"You'll have 365 pages by the end of a year: a whole novel!"—or who work in the midst of the full-throttle activity of their families, managing to crank out more in a week's time than many of us do in a few months.

In order to make the best use of our writing time, we need to innovate, so the more ideas about how to do this, the merrier. But these mentors' examples can lead us toward self-flagellating, a silly, absolutely counterproductive—and nearly irresistible—urge, spawning that unshakable inner voice that tells us whatever we're doing doesn't count.

We all know that voice. Sometimes it even does some good. It kicks our butts when we need it, makes us sit back down at the computer and slug out the next paragraph or chapter or stanza. Sometimes it even lifts our chins up after the fifth rejection letter in a row, reminds us of the beautiful places we go in our minds, of the importance of all forms of art in an increasingly regimented world, even gives us our ideas when we're not consciously thinking about our work, maybe when we're swimming in the ocean or reaching for laundry detergent at the grocery store.

But a lot of times we just need to tell that voice to shut the hell up. We need to tell it that what we're doing counts.

Say you're in the middle of working on a novel, but one day you get spirited away writing a short story instead. That counts! Even if it winds up being a lousy story and you throw it away later.

If you find yourself spending a few hours writing an essay about writing—a few hours that could've gone into revising a couple of stories that have been on your back burner so long there's a milky metaphorical scrim developing on the tops of them—that counts.

If you spend six hours one day writing and rewriting cover letters to help sell your stories / poems / novel, this is an essential part of the work we do. Writing those letters well makes the difference between our work being read or being tossed in the recycling bin, and the work we do distilling our grand notions into bite-sized "sales pitches" is some of the hardest writing around. So it counts.

If you spend your writing day watching documentaries and video blogs on Youtube about panic attacks because your main character has panic disorder and you're trying to learn as much as you can about it, that counts!

If you're working hard on a story or a book, and you come to a crossroads—do you kill off the main character or do you let her recover from the near fatal poisoning?—and you get up, put on some hiking shoes, set out for the great outdoors, and get think-think-thinking, sometimes, this yields your Great Answer. Sometimes, it doesn't. Both times, it counts.

So much of what we do as writers is not appreciated. The results from squishing our blood and souls into letters on a page so often remain inert, receiving rejection letters, never going out into the world to interact and change it in any way. Yet we toil on, undeterred for unfathomable, primal compulsions to communicate something ephemeral, something only we have to say.

So I'm skeptical of codified strategies for getting this mystical job done. I don't wake up at 5:00 a.m. I don't sit down for four hours in the same chair at the same time every day.

Because, sometimes, what I need to do is get up. I need to go out and mingle in the world, listen to the sounds of cars on rainy streets, eavesdrop on job interviews at the coffee shop, flip through channels of combative morning talk shows, lose myself in the weird world of the modern grocery store, exercise, look at mountains, watch birds fly. All of it informs what I do.

We're writers, and so we think the only time we're being writers is when we have a keyboard under our fingers or a pen in hand. But we're just as much writers when we're up and walking around, observing the world, reading a book, taking a walk, petting our cat. As long as we're intentional about our approach, then what we do counts.

160

Like Freud said about cigars, sometimes wasting time is just wasting time. But a lot of times, everything we're doing is part of the writing process. Learn to believe it, to use your fallow times, to ease up on self-punishment, and to love what you do. Because we need more writers and artists in this world, we really do.

(By the way, reading essays about writing—that counts, too!)

A Poem of Impact and Permanence

Lauvonda Lynn M. Young

(First Honorable Mention, 2013 Poetry Society of Virginia Adult Poetry Contest)

My tenure with John Donne's "Death Be Not Proud" has been a long one. I first became acquainted with Donne's poem in September 1955, when my brother, Jack Nelson, five years of age, died after a gunshot ripped open his chest. Jackie and my brother, Paul Edward, had been playing Cowboys and Indians. Paul decided it would be far more exciting to play with an uncle's rifle—one allegedly unloaded and secured in a locked shed. A single bullet produced a quick death. I was ten years old, learned enough to know the finality of death, but far too young to foresee the sadness that was going to cloak our family for the rest of our lives.

Prior to the founding of funeral chapels, viewings took place in homes. When I first heard the delivery of "Death Be Not Proud," I was standing beside my brother's casket in our overcrowded living room. Through the years I returned frequently to Donne's poem. Many times I included a copy of the poem in sympathy cards and in funeral announcements when I was responsible for making the arrangements for several family members. "Death Be Not Proud" was read and discussed in my college literature and creative writing classes.

I sifted through various interpretations and finally determined the poem's meaning, as it related to me. Donne's words tell me that death should not be feared, because even though the human body dies, the "Soul" lives forever. I take my understanding from the lines, "For, those whom thou think'st, thou dost overthrow," and "Die not, poor death, nor yet canst thou kill me." In the previous lines, Donne tells "Death" he may think he has won, but "Death" does not have the power to kill forever. In the next lines, "From rest and sleep, which but thy pictures be," and "Much pleasure, then from thee, much more must flow," Donne said the "picture" we see—that is the body in the coffin—merely is in a resting state. The "more to flow" gives credence to the belief the soul outlives the body. Donne amplified further by stating, "Rest of their bones, and soul's delivery," and "One short sleep past, we wake eternally." Donne meant the "bones" will "rest" in the shell of the human body, but the "Soul" continues to exist. In the final line of his poem, "And death shall be no more, death thou shalt die," Donne's words clearly state there will come a time when death, in the form we know it, no longer will exist.

Donne was a mortal, but his words help me believe in the possibility of an afterlife, even though I remain conflicted, since I am more spiritual than religious. The important thing to consider is that Donne's poem isn't primarily about religion. It is a poem of comfort. "Death Be Not Proud" wasn't written for the devoutly religious. Donne composed the poem to console all beings, be it an atheist, devout Christian, or me.

As I wait for the day when my death becomes reality, I will continue to derive solace in envisioning my brother, made whole again, waiting in a field of fragrance, ready to embrace me upon my arrival to the hereafter. In my vision, Jackie is five years old, but he has the wisdom of the wisest.

ABOUT THE AUTHORS

David Black ("Pop-Eye," poem), a retired English teacher and minister, is a former poetry editor of the *English Journal* and a frequent contributor of poems, essays, articles, and reviews to small magazines and academic journals, especially in the Appalachian region. He is the author of two books, *Some Task, Long Forgotten and Other Poems* and *The Clown in the Tent*, both from Persimmon Tree Press.

Lori Magai Dixon (special contributor; "Herculaneum," poem) took the long way around to writing. She pursues the craft in the Shenandoah Valley.

Phyllis Anne Duncan ("Meeting the Enemy," fiction) is a commercial pilot and former FAA safety official who lives and writes in the Shenandoah Valley of Virginia. Her short stories have been published in the collections *Blood Vengeance, Fences*, and *Spy Flash*. Her work has appeared in *eFiction Magazine*, in *The Blue Ridge Anthology 2013*, and in *1 Photo 50 Authors 100 Words*. She has studied writing at Gotham Writers Workshop, Writers.com, and Tinker Mountain Writers Workshop. She is a member of WriterHouse, James River Writers, Virginia Writers Club, Blue Ridge Writers, Shenandoah Valley Writers, SWAG Writers, and the Association of Writers and Writing Programs.

Justin Fike ("Caroline's Essential Emporium," fiction) grew up with a love for stories, from his grandmother's tales of her life on the South Dakota prairie to the Adventures of Robin Hood and more. He now channels that love into his novel in progress and variety of copyrighting and editing jobs. He recently received a Masters in Creative Writing from Oxford University. He currently lives in Staunton, Virginia, with his wife and a dog who believes he is a cat.

Cornelia Clay Fulghum ("Lovers," poem; "Why Certainty in Science Is Unscientific (or, Turning Richard Dawkins on His Head)," essay). It took me awhile to find my calling. I investigated academia, both as a student and teacher, including a mind-altering stint instructing Turkish students to speak English, as a member of the Peace Corps. Next it was journalism, in Atlanta and New York—and a job as a writer/editor with the Justice Department in Washington, D.C. Then I moved with my true love to the Blue Ridge Mountains, where we watch the foxes play out our back window. Now, at last, I've found my life's work—observing with wonder the follies and grandeur of life, in both poetry and prose.

Jody Hobbs Hesler (special contributor; "The Famous Poet's Umbrella," fiction; "Feedback: Where to Draw the Line" "What Counts," writing) lives and writes in the foothills of the Blue Ridge Mountains. Her work has appeared or is forthcoming in *Stealing Time: A Literary Magazine for Parents*, *Valpariaso Fiction Review*, *Prime Number*, *Pearl*, *The Blue Ridge Anthology*, *Writer's Eye Anthology*, *Potato Eyes Journal*, *Leaf Garden Press*, *Charlottesville Family Magazine*, *Steel Toe Review*, and *A Short Ride: Remembering Barry Hannah*. One of her stories was nominated for a Pushcart Prize. Others have won local and regional contests. She has been a fellow in residence at the Virginia Center for the Creative Arts and has attended Juniper Summer Writing Institute and Sewanee and Bread Loaf Writers' Conferences.

Sarah Collins Honenberger ("Fishing," fiction; "Yet Another Massacre," poem). Sarah Honenberger's novel, *Catcher, Caught*, is a Pen/Faulkner Foundation selection for its Writers-in-Schools program. Audio and German editions were released in October 2012. With numerous fiction awards and a fellowship from the Virginia Center for the Creative Arts, she appears regularly on literary panels and at book festivals. Her other novels include *Waltzing Cowboys* and *White Lies: A Tale of Babies, Vaccines and Deception*, both nominees for the Library of Virginia Fiction Award. Her manuscript, *Minding Henry Lewis*, was a finalist in the 2013 Best Unpublished Novel Contest, and she has been a multiple placer in *The HooK* short story contest. A former president of the Blue Ridge Writers Chapter of the Virginia Writers Club, she now lives and writes from her Rappahannock River home.

Gary D. Kessler ("Joleen Finds Her Voice," fiction; "I Hit a Deer," poem; "The Day Anastasia Ticked Off Rasputin's Daughter," essay), a freelance book editor, is a former news agency managing editor, diplomat, newspaper columnist, and movie consultant. His published works include a short story collection, *On the Downtown Mall*; volume editor for the two-volume *WritersNet Anthology of Prose* and the four-volume *Blue Ridge Anthology*; coauthor of a publishing reference, *Finding Go! Matching Questions and Resources in Getting Published*; and a mystery novel, *What the Spider Saw*, which was nominated for the Library of Virginia Fiction Award. He has won or placed in VWC annual contests, the UVa Art Museum's Writer's Eye prose contest, and *The HooK* short story contest. His poetry has appeared in the *Piedmont Virginian*. He also writes pen name mystery novellas and novels.

Phyllis R. Koch-Sheras, PhD ("Lost . . . and Found," poem; "Mother of the Bride," essay) is a clinical psychologist and author, living and working in Charlottesville since 1974. She has coauthored several books, including *The Dream Sourcebook*, *Couple Power Therapy: Building Commitment, Cooperation, Communication and Community in Relationships*, and *Lifelong Love: Creating and Maintaining an Extraordinary Relationship*. Currently, she is writing a musical entitled "Therapy: the Musical." Phyllis is also a professional opera singer and watercolor artist. She has had several solo art exhibits in Charlottesville, which include poetry readings of her poems inspired by the paintings. She is married and has two grown children.

Jean Lancaster (special contributor; "Taking the Waters," essay) is a Richmond native who lives in Charlottesville. Two of her nonfiction works are published in *The Blue Ridge Anthology 2013*. Her daughter's courage inspired her first published work "Shattered." Her short story "Tantilla" earned first place in the Blue Ridge Writers Chapter annual contest and second place in the Virginia Writers Club competition in 2013. Her writing voice evolved during research of ancestors who were English settlers of Flowerdew Hundred Plantation, French Huguenots of Manakintown, and nineteenth-century Presbyterian missionaries to China. With aspirations of becoming a "Southern" author, she has written a stream of short stories and nonfiction essays.

Susan M. Lanterman (special contributor; "The Most Fragile Gift," essay) writes human-interest stories for the Commentary section of *The Daily Progress* newspaper and has coauthored "On the Block," a real estate column published in *The HooK* newspaper. While in New Hampshire, she produced PC Connection's Guide and edited the Mary Hitchcock Memorial Newsletter. Upon moving to Charlottesville, she managed the online journal *Neurosurgical Focus* for the *Journal of Neurosurgery* for nine years. Susan is currently completing a young adult novel, "Hasta Luego, Santa Claus," which follows the antics of a teenager and his family of illegal immigrants. She is also writing a collection of short stories based on her Charlottesville B&B.

Linda Levokove ("The African Queen," essay) is the author of two books of poetry, *Walk On The Heart Side* and *Cabbages & Kings*. She was docent educator at the UVa Art Museum, teaches poetry classes, is past vice president of the Blue Ridge Writers Chapter of the Virginia Writers Club, and is a member of the Poetry Society of Virginia and the Virginia Writers Club, which has presented her with a special award for outstanding service and contribution to poetry in Central Virginia. Linda has read at and moderated panels at the Virginia Festival of the Book. She is presently writing a collection of short stories.

Sigrid Mirabella ("Night Moths," poem), originally from Long Island, New York, defines herself as a social hermit and hopeful skeptic living in rural uncertainty. Her works have won awards and have appeared in *The Blue Ridge Anthology, Mid-America Poetry Review, Long Island Pet Gazette, Lynchburg News and Advance, Dog Fancy, Woman's Day, Countryside, People Magazines,* and various Macmillan/Howell books. In her other life, she works for a humane society in Nelson County, Virginia.

Deborah M. Prum (special contributor; "Escape," fiction; "Don't Iron Your Clothes While They're on Your Body No Matter How Late You Are," writing) is the author of *Fatty in the*

Back Seat (a young adult novel), *First Kiss and Other Cautionary Tales* (an audiobook collection of humorous essays that first aired on NPR-member stations), *Czars and Czarinas* (an anecdotal and interactive history in iBook format) and *Rats, Bulls and Flying Machines* (a print book about the Renaissance). Her award-winning short fiction has been published in many places, including the *The Virginia Quarterly Review, The Blue Ridge Anthology,* and *The Sweetbay Review.* Her humorous essays appear in print and air on NPR-member stations. Her work can be seen at www.deborahprum.com.

Elaine Ruggieri ("Playing Nightly," fiction), former vice president of public relations at the University of Virginia's Darden School of Business, has lived in Albemarle County since 1964. Writing nonfiction prose throughout her career, she is now concentrating on fiction. Her short story, "Deep Quarry," was published in *The Blue Ridge Anthology 2009*, and "Doomsday" and the poem, "Lost in Verse," in *The Blue Ridge Anthology 2013*.

Marilou Schunter (special contributor; "Radishes and Roses Café" and "Poppies in the Dining Room," poems) lives in Culpeper, Virginia. Her poetry has been published in the photography book, *The Blue Ridge Parkway Celebration*; the *Piedmont Virginian* magazine; *The Blue Ridge Anthology 2013* and *2011*; *Arizona: 100 Years, 100 Poems, 100 Poets*; and Windmore writer's anthology, *Touching the Heart*. She recently received an Honorable Mention Award for her poem "Radishes and Roses Café" in the Fralin Museum of Art's 27th Writer's Eye Poetry and Prose Competition. In the mid-1990s she wrote two columns, one called "Hello Marilou" in *Culpeper*, the magazine, and a family column in the *Culpeper-Star Exponent*. She chaired Windmore's Brown Bag Poetry Contest for ten years and has taught poetry in Culpeper's After School Arts Program. Ms. Schunter is currently a member of the Blue Ridge Writers and Lonesome Mountain Prose Workshop.

Elizabeth Doyle Solomon ("Roses Remember," poem), a New Orleans native and retired teacher, began writing at age eleven and publishing at age thirteen. At age seventy-one, she reckons her poems total over 60,000. Elizabeth has published two poetry collections, *Seasons* and *The Steering Wheel Poems*, written newspaper columns, and founded the *Central Virginia Leader* newspaper. Her recent awards for both poetry and prose have come from the Poetry Society of Virginia and the Blue Ridge Writers. She leads the Blue Ridge weekly poets' critique group and is preparing a third book for publication, *Journey West and Everywhere.*

Olivia Stowe (volume editor; "Moment of the Deer," fiction) lives and writes in Central Virginia. Stowe's specialty is cozy mystery novellas, which include a thus-far eight-volume series of Charlotte Diamond mysteries, the most recent of which was *Horrid Honeymoon.* The Christmas-season short story, "Cassandra's Last Spotlight," adds to this series. Stowe's standalone mysteries include *Fiddler's Rest* and *Restoration of the Castle*, and inspirational Christmas short story collections are available in the *Spirit of Christmas* and *Christmas Seconds* anthologies.

Jack Trammell ("St. Paul's Illumination," fiction; "The Master's Touch," poem) lives on a farm in Central Virginia, where he is a modern agrarian and a recognized voice of Appalachia (born in Berea, Kentucky). His writing credits are diverse, ranging from hundreds of poems, articles, and stories to larger book-length projects and academic research related to his college teaching. He is a trained historian, a research methodologist, and an environmental advocate, but most of all he is committed to the act and art of writing, as well as encouraging others in their personal literary journeys. He can be reached at jacktrammell@yahoo.com.

Leonard Tuchyner ("Herbie the Beet," fiction; "Emergency Operation," essay) is a semiretired counselor, who lives in Central Virginia with his wife and two dogs. He maintains an active involvement in the local writing community, which includes participation in two writing critique groups and in the Blue Ridge Writers Club. Although challenged by legal blindness, he continues to pursue Tai Chi and related forms of martial arts.

Gardening is another passion that has captivated him for most of his seventy-three-year-old life. One of his most fulfilling endeavors is the facilitation of a Senior Center's Writing for Healing and Growth writing group. He has been in the winners' circle of the Blue Ridge Writers Club's yearly writing contest several times. His winning entries have included poetry, fiction, and nonfiction. He has also been a regular contributor to *The Blue Ridge Anthology*. Mr. Tuchyner has published essays, poetry, and short stories in *Dialogue Magazine*, *Magnets and Ladders*, *Nomad's Choir*, and *Westward Quarterly*. His first poetry book is soon to be published.

Marvin Loyd Welborn ("an essence of being," poem) blew in out of the West and settled into Central Virginia in 1979. He worked in the international banking trade for thirty years and retired to writing poetry in Charlottesville, Virginia. His first published book, *Union Station and Paradigm Shift*, was published in 2012. His poetry has been included in *The dVerse Anthology: Voices of Contemporary World Poetry*, and he is currently at work on another book "Tales of the Tribe," to be publish in the spring of 2014. His Web site is www.tinkwelborn.com.

Lauvonda Lynn M. Young (special contributor; "Second Encounter," fiction; "A Poem of Impact and Permanence," poem), past president of the Blue Ridge Writers Chapter of the Virginia Writers Club, is author of *Just a Woman* and has poems published in various sources, including *Young America Sings, National High School Anthology*, the *Piedmont Virginian*, and *Blue Ridge Parkway Celebration, Silver Anniversary Edition*. Her winning poetry includes the Poetry Guild's Editor's Choice Award for "Flowers" (*Shelter in the Storm*, 1998); second place for "Gardening" (*The Blue Ridge Anthology 2009*); and "My Papa Was a Coal Miner" (Poetry Society of Virginia, 2011). Former editor of two newsletters, *The Blue Ridge* and *Friends Focus*, Lynn has authored newspaper articles in *The College Newspaper, Senior Center Times*, and the *Fluvanna Review*. She is a reviewer for Shepard University's *Anthology of Appalachian Writers*.

www.ingramcontent.com/pod-product-compliance
Lightning Source LLC
Chambersburg PA
CBHW051518170626
46811CB00002B/891